THIS IS BEYOND

ALSO BY EVAN TSITSIAS

The Directors Lab: Techniques, Methods, and Conversations About All Things Theatre (editor)

ALSO BY BILAL BAIG

Acha Bacha
Eraser (with Sadie Epstein-Fine, Christol Bryan, Marina Gomes, Yousef Kadoura, Tijiki Morris, Anthony Perpuse, and Nathan Redburn)

THIS IS BEYOND

A TIME CAPSULE OF QUEER EXPERIENCE

EDITED BY EVAN TSITSIAS AND BILAL BAIG

PLAYWRIGHTS CANADA PRESS
TORONTO

First edition: December 2023
Printed and bound in Canada by Imprimerie Gauvin, Gatineau

Jacket art and design by Tim Singleton

Playwrights Canada Press
202-269 Richmond St. W., Toronto, ON M5V 1X1
416.703.0013 | info@playwrightscanada.com | www.playwrightscanada.com

LIBRARY AND ARCHIVES CANADA CATALOGUING IN PUBLICATION
Title: This is beyond : a time capsule of queer experience / edited by Evan Tsitsias and Bilal Baig.
Names: Tsitsias, Evan, editor. | Baig, Bilal, editor.
Description: Poetry, plays, and essays.
Identifiers: Canadiana 20230540848 | ISBN 9780369104731 (softcover)
Subjects: LCSH: Gay theater—Canada. | LCSH: Homosexuality in the theater—Canada. | LCSH: Canadian drama—21st century—History and criticism. | CSH: Canadian drama (English)—21st century—History and criticism.
Classification: LCC PS8169.H6 T55 2023 | DDC C812.009/35266—dc23

Playwrights Canada Press staff work across Turtle Island, on Treaty 7, Treaty 13, and Treaty 20 territories, which are the current and ancestral homes of the Anishinaabe Nations (Ojibwe / Chippewa, Odawa, Potawatomi, Algonquin, Saulteaux, Nipissing, and Mississauga / Michi Saagiig), the Blackfoot Confederacy (Kainai, Piikani, and Siksika), néhiyaw, Sioux, Stoney Nakoda, Tsuut'ina, Wendat, and members of the Haudenosaunee Confederacy (Mohawk, Oneida, Onondaga, Cayuga, Seneca, and Tuscarora), as well as Metis and Inuit peoples. It always was and always will be Indigenous land.

We acknowledge the financial support of the Canada Council for the Arts, the Ontario Arts Council (OAC), Ontario Creates, the Government of Ontario, and the Government of Canada for our publishing activities.

To that kid, or that wanderer somewhere, who feels misunderstood, unseen, unheard, unsure, or absolutely sure. Hope you find a kindred spirit inside this book. We see you.

TABLE OF CONTENTS

CHAPTER 5: EXPOSED

CHAPTER 6: TOUCH BUT DON'T TELL

PREFACE

EVAN TSITSIAS AND BILAL BAIG

The following was our call for submissions for this anthology:

> We invite you to submit monologues for publication in an anthology, a collection of monologues for 2SLGBTQ+ and non-binary voices. This book aims to gather monologues that reflect a breadth of themes, styles, cultures, and creative practices across generations and borders.
>
> The goal of this book is to create a canon of monologues that reflect what it means to be queer or on the spectrum of the 2SLGBTQ+ community through a modern lens, while chronicling and championing as many diverse voices as possible. We are curious about the future of queer theatre. The intersections of queerness and cultures. Post–AIDS stories. Have we moved past "coming out" stories, or are those inherent inside every queer person's story? What are new, unexpected things we find ourselves coming out about? What isn't being talked about enough in our communities? What happens to our stories when we give ourselves the permission to write about whatever we want? We want to give voice to what it means to be a member of this community in this ever-evolving world, allowing actors of every age, colour, culture, and generation something to play with, ponder, learn, and recite. This includes featuring work from writers who identify as any of the following: 2/Two-Spirit, gay, lesbian, bisexual, transgender, non-binary, queer, genderqueer, questioning, intersex, asexual, pangender, agender, bigender, gender variant. We hope to contribute and respond to what is happening around the world today. We want to be inspired, moved, confronted, provoked, educated, shocked, and called into action.

That was what we initially were aiming for. What we received were hundreds of stunning submissions, crammed with the guts and the glorious gore of brave souls, candidly sharing their stories and filling our inbox. It became so much more than we had anticipated. Confusion, expectation, grief, moments of joy, grace and redemption, countless questions, and other investigations emerged. Questions we had never anticipated. Stories that were capturing a specific time we are all experiencing. We wanted to know more as we continued to curate. We wanted more than solely monologues that could be performed. So we decided to invite several playwrights and academics to write "opinion" pieces, charting and chronicling their thoughts on the evolution of queer theatre through their own personal lens and experiences. These we've interspersed amongst the monologues. This anthology became more than we originally predicted. We strove to create a time capsule. To chronicle a moment in history when seismic change is occurring both on and off stage. What was similarly illuminating was the experimentation of form and structure these writers used in their work. Poetry, prose, heightened language, stream of consciousness, and more all synthesized and opened up new gateways into these stories.

Over the last few years there's been a disturbance. A rupture of the equilibrium to which the world has been accustomed. Gender has changed. Evolved. New vernacular. New voices. What an exciting time to capture for our community. We hoped to offer a space for those voices we might not have heard much from in the past. We aimed to find the intersections of queerness and cultures that would open up the horizons of the readers. Marginalized voices that have felt silenced.

We've divided these monologues into thematic chapters, whether it be reflections of youth (Before), sexual encounters (Touch But Don't Tell), stories of discovery, sometimes shocking ourselves (Trigger Warning), moments of epiphanies and truths (Anagnorisis), and more.

We hope these stories widen your own lens and open up your mind to reflect on the glorious spectrum of the queer community and the stark truths that exist within it. We've come a long way, but even as we write this preface, the world once again is seeing an onslaught of violence and hate for our community. We have to ask ourselves how it's possible that we can continue to have these same conversations. That people still think we are dangerous. Well, maybe we are. But for all the right reasons. Because we are resilient. Because we refuse to back off. Because we continue to disrupt. To provoke. To change. To evolve. Hopefully this book will be a tiny part of the provocation and the evolution. We must continue to tell our stories. It's our duty.

If not us, then who?

INTRODUCTION

EVAN TSITSIAS

Queer. What a word. It sends instant chills through my body. It elicits thoughts of it being screamed out the window of a passing car, or a whisper under someone's breath as they pass. A simple word to remind us who we are. Who they think we are. Our place in this world. You only need to be called queer in public once to understand that level of shame and humiliation. You'll do anything to prevent it from happening again. You'll avoid eye contact. You'll dress in a way to divert any unwanted attention. You'll "accidentally" bump your hand against your partner's so you feel safe to touch in public. Well, I'm speaking for myself. And that's why I've struggled with this word for so long.

When the idea for this book was born, it was a direct response to what was happening in the world at the time. Non-binary, genderfluid, genderqueer, gender performance, and similar terms were thankfully becoming part of society's vernacular. Terms that never existed or seemed available in my own youth were now being used by a new generation with a stunning ease that I never had the privilege of incorporating into my vocabulary or description of self. I've ruminated upon these words and negotiated them in my mind for a long time. I wondered how these terms would have affected me as a child. What would have changed? *Would* anything have changed? Who would I be now?

When I was young, people would always ask me if I was a boy or a girl. I think it was a combination of my androgynous looks and my demeanour. Whatever it was, it made me question gender and how it applied to me from a very young age. I felt like I had a secret. There was a period of time that I thought I might be a girl. I wasn't sure why. I am not sure if I wanted to be a girl or if I didn't want to be a boy, to be honest. I'm not sure I knew the difference. But it was there, buried deep in me. I definitely felt the "performance" of my gender even as a child, especially because I felt staggeringly unsuccessful at it. It made me almost mute, afraid of opening my mouth or uttering a word. Afraid of seeing people's eyes widen in that moment of recognition or shock. "Oh, he's that way?" I certainly was. So I studied girls on the subway, the bus, the street. I'd pick up some of their mannerisms and try them out in the privacy of my bathroom mirror. I liked the way they fit on me and inside me. But I knew I could never explore that outside the bathroom. I knew what would happen, even at nine years old. Even though I never knew the word "queer" then, I knew what it felt like to *be* that word. Peculiar. My behaviour in the bathroom was peculiar. It still is. Which is why my relationship with the word "queer" is deep and fraught with tension, miscommunication, and sordid history. I've wrestled with it. Interrogated it. I've monitored its evolution in tandem with my own personal revolution over the years. "Queer" is marginalized. It sounds dangerous. It's completely "othered." That word carries immense historical and emotional baggage. It elicits painful memories being used as a slur hurled at me in my childhood to inflict pain and shame. I looked it up in the dictionary. It means "odd, peculiar, abnormal, differing in some way from what is usual." Its synonyms are "crazy, disquieting, eccentric, funny, irrational, irregular, oddball, puzzling." Puzzling indeed. All these things I felt like as a child, but never understood why. If we are what we eat, are we also what we read? Are all those words who I am? The subversion of this word, like many other pejorative euphemisms the world has reclaimed, has wreaked havoc on my sometimes delicate psyche. To navigate this word in a modern context takes its toll both mentally, emotionally, and spiritually.

Like many theatre artists, I started off my theatrical career as an actor, playing roles I never wanted to play—mainly straight males. I unfortunately started performing when queer roles were nascent, few and far between. I quickly grew tired of pretending to be straight on stage since I spent most of my life to that point doing the same. I was sick of receiving notes from teachers or casting directors to be "less animated." God, how I hated that. Just say "Stop acting so gay!" and get on with it. I wanted to speak words that meant something to me. I did have those opportunities at times, but this was the '90s and we were only beginning to see these shows emerge featuring queer characters. Or at least that's what it felt like to me. So I stopped performing and began writing and directing, hoping to tell the stories that felt relevant to me, that would resonate with my community. Then one day, a friend (with good intentions) asked me why everything I wrote was about something "gay." I instantly felt shamed and humiliated and, again, not sure why. My default, and I think a lot of queer people's, is to blame ourselves. Now I wish I had shouted, "I write about gay people because I am gay!" But alas, no. I went home with my tail between my legs and started to write about anyone and everyone else. Gay men cloaked in women characters who spoke their words. I wanted to write about being queer.

But what does it mean to be queer? What does it mean to be queer on stage? I'm certainly no expert, but I want to pose those questions to you. Recently this idea of audience "voyeurism" has emerged. The theory that audiences are drawn to trauma inflicted on certain marginalized groups as a way to covertly watch atrocities being inflicted upon bodies that aren't their own from the safety of their seats. It's a fascinating subconscious remnant of our programming throughout our lives. We've been trained to watch disenfranchised groups suffer and, in turn, be "entertained" by the act of watching it through the safe lens of art. Which brings me to my next question . . . Who are we making queer theatre for?

There is oftentimes an unconscious bias that we carry for groups we are not part of, and it's veiled in seemingly innocuous words or interpretations. I think of the gay characters, both overt and covert, I was exposed to as a child and the value I put on myself as a result of what and who I was watching. There seemed to be a vilification of queer characters in almost everything. I began to question how queer characters were being represented on stage, even by queer creators, including myself. How do we impose our own biases into the characters we see and create? How can we be aware of it? Now that I've located that as something to be cognizant of when both watching and creating queer characters, the interrogation of these personalities is of huge interest and concern to me. I'm now consciously observing when they are used as vehicles as the brunt of the joke, sometimes their own. Or when they are relegated to the role of the clown or the pariah, the best friend or the sarcastic one, the intellectual quippy one or the cynical nasty one, and the list goes on and on. Most times, their arc ends in some type of catastrophe. Perhaps death. Or they completely vanish after they are no longer of service to their straight counterpart. Where does stereotype intrude, and is it our responsibility to dismantle that stereotype even when (though oftentimes it's hard to admit) it sometimes exists?

Every time I watch a show, I chart the path of the queer roles. What do they say? What is said about them? How are they used in the piece? How is the audience responding? If it's a straight audience, what do they laugh at? What do they feel when they watch queer trauma? If we are writing queer characters for straight audiences, what are we telling them about us? How much do we reveal? Where are the stories of queer joy? Are audiences interested in those stories? I offer this series of questions to you as we all navigate this new terrain of queer stories that are evolving rapidly nowadays.

It's heartening to see how queer roles are being redefined in theatre currently. I've noticed a definite shift in the stories that are being told. Queer characters are no longer simply on the sidelines, but instead in the main narrative. Joyful, defiant, resilient, and three-dimensional. The submissions we received galvanized these thoughts with their candor and the stories they told. I've learned so much reading from inside the spectrum of queer narratives. My lens has widened not only from the stories themselves but also from the structure in which they are being written. I've had to deprogram my own bias in what I've been taught is "classic structure" and be open to new forms that are emerging.

The journey of creating this book with Bilal and reading through the stunning submissions we received has offered me some true healing, and I think (though I'm still not positive) that I can now safely use the word "queer" to describe myself as a member of the 2SLGBTQ+ community. Queer was something I desperately tried to avoid being my entire life, but now I think I love it. I think I *am* it. I am queer. In all its twisted and loaded glory.

The pendulum has begun to swing in our direction. Let's hope it never swings back to the other side. We hope this anthology can contribute to the evolution of queer stories on all our stages. We created this anthology to celebrate how far we've come, to grieve together for what we still can't say or do. It's a stew of memories and thoughts and theories. Recording our history matters. We are living in our future history and this anthology will capture a capsule in time of this present. By the time it's finally published and in your hands, who knows what will have changed. But that is the exciting part, this rapid moment of evolution we find ourselves in, when everything is exposed, interrogated, investigated. When we are left to define ourselves in our own way and with our own voice. Which is exactly how it should be.

CHAPTER 1
BEFORE

INSTRUCTIONS FOR THE INVOCATION OF YOUR QUEER ANCESTORS

ADAM MEISNER

Adam Meisner (he/they) writes plays, poetry, and fiction. Adam's most recent play, *For Both Resting and Breeding*, about a genderless society in the year 2150, premiered at Talk Is Free Theatre in Barrie, Ontario, in 2018. The company subsequently toured the play to Australia in early 2020 and to Argentina and Chile in 2023. Scirocco Drama published *For Both Resting and Breeding* in 2023.

In this stand-alone monologue, a speaker presents a set of instructions for how to invoke the presence of one's queer ancestors—an opportunity for queer people who are alive today to connect with their queer forebearers whose lives and legacies have been obscured by received histories. The piece was inspired by a project by visual artists AA Bronson and Peter Hobbs titled "Invocation of the Queer Spirits."

This piece was written without a named character ("The Speaker") to allow a variety of queer actors to perform the part and interpret it according to the many ways a person can be queer. The actor has the opportunity to give the Speaker a name, either the actor's real name or a name they have invented for the character.

✦✦✦

THE SPEAKER stands in a wooded corner of a public park with a large canvas bag over one shoulder that is filled with props for the instructions that follow.

THE SPEAKER: First, you must find the perfect place—ideally somewhere public that feels private. This wooded corner of a park is a good example, but you could also use a quiet study room in a university library or a vacant stall in a public-transit restroom.

Wherever you choose, you should arrive at a dim hour: either early in the morning or late in the evening. Too much light and no spirits will show up; too much darkness and you might summon the ghosts of your blood relations—and this is an exercise to invoke your queer ancestors, who are of no real relation, but who are, in every way, more related to you than genetic kin.

Next, you'll need to make your setting as inviting as possible. I recommend a picnic blanket—something as bright as a luminous gemstone, like lapis lazuli, but also as soft as a carpet of rock cap moss.

The SPEAKER pulls out a blanket from their canvas bag, spreads it out, and starts to set up for a picnic as they deliver the following lines:

I recommend you decorate your blanket with the usual accoutrements for a picnic. You might put out a few plates of food: finger sandwiches, chips and dip, crudité, that sort of thing. The spirits like snacks as much as we do.

If the sun is setting, a candle or two won't hurt—but please nothing that recalls a church. This should feel more seductive than spiritual.

The SPEAKER *lies down.*

Recline on your side as if you've just finished eating and you feel sleepy with the weight of the food in your belly—but not so sleepy that you'd turn down a little romp.

The SPEAKER *stares seductively at their audience.*

Now soften your gaze as you look off into the distance. As far as the eye can see. Then look beyond that point—without squinting—and breathe.

A deepening tranquility.

Focus on the sound of your breathing. Allow it to hypnotize you. Allow it to soften your gaze even more. Allow it to bring you to the brink of sleep and then, when you are so relaxed you feel as if you might sink into the ground—

The SPEAKER *sits up, suddenly alert.*

Say your name. Say it fast. Say it slow. Say it as if it has new peaks and valleys. Say it so that you find new words within your name, new names within your name. Say it as if it contains multitudes. Say it so many times that it starts to sound funny—so that it starts to sound as queer as it possibly can.

My name is [the Speaker inserts their name here, either their actual name or a name made up for their character], and I will say my name as many times as needed to make the spirits come.

The SPEAKER *says their name over and over—perhaps nearly thirty times—varying the pace, cadence, and inflections. At some point, the pace quickens, almost to a climax, and then stops as they notice something in the distance. Maybe drum music starts to play, or the sound of shuffling feet can be heard—distant at first, but getting closer and louder, almost unbearably loud over the next few lines.*

There they are. Do you see them? Marching down from the skies. Oh, look at them in the majesty of their brilliant parade. They're coming—they're coming—are you ready? They're—here.

A haunted look on the SPEAKER*'s face followed by an elated silence.*

Welcome, all you magnificent beings. I thought you'd never get here. Come! Gather round and tell me what I need to know to continue what you began.

Blackout.

HARUN

MAKRAM AYACHE

Makram Ayache is an award-winning playwright, performer, director, and educator living between Alberta and Toronto. His playwriting explores representations of queer Arab voices and aims to bridge political struggles and the intimate experiences of the people impacted by them. The 2023 world premiere of Ayache's *The Hooves Belonged to the Deer* (Tarragon Theatre with Buddies in Bad Times Theatre) was described as "the most excitingly theatrical piece of new writing to premiere in Toronto" by the *Globe and Mail* and garnered a critics' pick. Previously, *The Green Line* (Downstage and Chromatic Theatre) garnered four Betty Mitchell Award nominations, winning two, including for Outstanding New Play. Ayache is the recipient of the 2020 Tom Hendry Award for *Harun*. He has also been nominated for four Elizabeth Sterling Haynes Awards for his plays *Harun* (2018) and *The Green Line* (2019) in Edmonton, Alberta. Alongside writing, Ayache directs and performs, most recently working alongside Mitchell Cushman as associate director for Outside the March and Factory Theatre's production of *Trojan Girls* by Gillian Clark. Currently, he is developing *Small Gods (at the Start of the World)* with support from Toronto's Factory Theatre and working on his first graphic novel project. Explore his work at www.makramayache.com.

After Harun's mother discovers he's gay, she is killed in a tragic accident. A year later, Harun is struck with a dystopian vision and a wilting angel comes to him with a dire warning. As he and his friends organize a campus protest against a white-supremacist uprising, bad turns to worse as the veil between the political and the spiritual thins. Reality blurs with spiritual revelation in this tale of an immigrant Arab Canadian navigating his sexuality in Canada.

Harun's visions have hit a fever pitch. He has become negligent and emotionally distant from his friends. He has become unpredictable and rageful against his boyfriend. He is alone, unsure where to turn. He has avoided processing his feelings of his mother's death, and now he sits with his demons.

Harun was first produced by In Arms Theatre Collective in Edmonton, Alberta, on August 15, 2018. It was performed by Jacob Holloway, Sarah J. Culkin, Hillary Warden, Griffin Cork, Amena Shehab, and Makram Ayache; directed by Mieko Ouchi; with stage management by Jessica Haggeman; production design by Reza Basirzadeh; lighting design by Caro Vanrensberg; and sound design by Chris Pereira.

✦ HARUN'S DEMONS ✦

HARUN: When I was a little kid I would have a hard time falling asleep because I was afraid of the dark. Sometimes I'd go to the edge of my mom's bed and gently shake her awake.
I'd ask, "Mom, when will it be morning?"
She'd say, "Heyete *[sweetheart]*, just close your eyes and go back to sleep, it'll be morning soon."

I'd do as she said but I could still see their faces: the witches and ghouls of my imagination, who stood, with their toothy grins, at the edge of my bed, watching . . . waiting.
I used to hear the shallow breathing of a ghost child who abruptly went away one day when I confronted him. I said, "What do you want?!" And I never heard from him again.

Now I miss that ghost child and his cryptic breathing because I grew up, queer and disoriented, and the fears of adulthood proved more fearful than those playful fairytale creatures. Now I long to dance with the witches and demons, swim in lakes of fire with devils, and listen to the silence of ghosts. Because the monsters today are layered and internal. They are slivers of glass churning in your stomach. They're an insect burrowing in your skull. They are a bomb at an airport. They are a truck plowing through a crowd. They are a massacre at a club.

They are hate incarnate.
And they are in you.
And they are in me.
I can no longer gently shake her awake and ask, "Mom, when will it be morning?" She can offer me no promises of sunlight in this sunless apocalypse.

And when you keep company with demons, the lines blur between where they end and you begin.

THE KISSING GAME

RHIANNON COLLETT

Rhiannon Collett (they/them) is a playwright, performer, and translator based in Vancouver on the territories of the Squamish, Musqueam, and Tsleil-Waututh Nations. They are interested in interdisciplinary creation processes, sexual labour, gender performativity, and science fiction. Selected playwriting credits include *Miranda & Dave Begin Again* (Playwrights Guild of Canada's RBC Emerging Playwright Award), *Wasp* (Nightswimming/safeword), *The Kissing Game* (Youtheatre/Young People's Theatre/Maison Théâtre), *J'ai Jamais* (French translation by Pénélope Bourque, Youtheatre/Télé-Québec/Maison Théâtre), and *Girlfriend* (Young People's Theatre).

Kate and Sam are best friends, but there's a tension building in their relationship. When Kate's sister falls victim to an act of violence, they are determined to bring the perpetrator to justice. On a summer evening, their actions tear a hole in reality as the assailant's heart falls out of his chest and onto the pavement, just as it begins to snow. Their relationship crumbles in the aftermath and the girls are left to question whether any of us are truly worthy of forgiveness.

Sam tells us about her father's betrayal, and the beginning of her friendship with Kate.

The Kissing Game was first produced by Youtheatre in Montréal on November 27, 2018. It was performed by Rhiannon Collett, directed and dramaturged by Michel Lefebvre, with stage management by Frédérique Folly, assistant stage management by Tori Morrison, lightning and set design by Martin Sirois, and sound design by Sara Magnan. The play was originally published by Éditions La Bagnole in 2023.

✦✦✦

SAM: It starts like this.

Kate moves into town with her older sister, Frankie. I immediately notice her because she's kind of weird and really pretty and always alone. Like, constantly alone. We're in the same homeroom and I watch her out of the corner of my eye for like six months before I finally work up the nerve to say hi. I don't usually talk to anyone, because it seems like a lot of effort but . . . Kate is different. Her hair is always ratty and wild and she wears these bright lipsticks that get kind of smeared in the corner of her mouth, or on her teeth, like she can try all she wants to be perfect but she knows it isn't gonna work. Her sister, Frankie, is four years older than her but they're best friends. She has lots of tattoos and piercings and she almost always wears sunglasses. Sometimes Frankie comes and picks Kate up from school and they walk home together, smoking. People always look at them but nobody ever says anything. Kate and Frankie are cool. Like. They probably don't even have parents. That's how cool they are. They just appeared one day on the planet like fully formed people.

I'm sure you can tell, but I'm not cool like that. I have parents, and my twin brother Roger and they seem to cling to me like people can see how embarrassing they are even when they're not there.

We live in a rickety house by the train tracks; I like to get up really early and watch the sun rise up over the railway. If you're there at the right time, everything turns gold and the tracks become this sea you can walk on. I steal my dad's cigarettes from his coat by the door and smoke two or three before school. He pretends like he doesn't notice, but there's always a fresh pack. It's like we're talking when we're not. My dad's not big into feelings, so I take what closeness I can get.

Then, about a year after Kate and Frankie pull into our neighbourhood, his coat goes missing. It's not by the door, it's not over the couch, it's not on a chair in the kitchen. It's not in the bathroom or out back or forgotten on the front step. It's just . . . gone. No note, no nothing. No smokes.

My dad's gone too. Obviously. And he doesn't come back. For three months.

I start getting twitchy. At school, all I can think about is having a cig. I'm not careful when I look at Kate anymore, she sees me watching. I'm easily embarrassed. I bite my nails, pick at my skin, go for nervous walks around the block by myself at lunch. I give myself a pep talk, but I end up just muttering "suck it up, bitch, suck it up!!! Suck it UP! Don't you dare cry" until I'm weeping and late to class and I have to apologize to myself. I give up on last period, and I'm sitting on the back steps by the ravine, when Kate approaches me. She's wearing smudged purple lipstick and she looks me dead in the eyes before speaking. For a moment it seems like we've been friends for ages.

"Do you want a cigarette," she says.

I accept.

Kate and I hit it off. We hang out every single day. We roll our eyes in unison in class. We share lipstick. We eat lunch together. When we have a free period, we go to Tim Hortons and steal creamers. We have a competition to see how many we can pocket and Kate wins by shoving them all down the front of her overalls. In Law class, she drinks the creamers one by one, slowly, luxuriously, so that by the end of the period a castle of tiny plastic cups has appeared on her desk. She stares the teacher down when he looks to say something, and then he shrugs and lets us go early. She always has her homework done. It's always right. She's always late, but she gets by. Kate moves in her own time and the school obliges. I take her home for dinner and she sleeps over and I see my brother Roger looking at her brushing her teeth in the bathroom. He tells her she's pretty and she tells him to cut it out.

The next week we're in Biology and I feel like I'm going to die I'm so goddamn bored. Mr. MacLean keeps droning on and on and on, and Kate kicks my chair and I'm like, what? And she's like . . . "Do you wanna?" Do I wanna what? And then she goes snip snip snip with her fingers.

So we'd been talking. A lot. About my hair. And somehow Kate decides that today, at 1:42 p.m. is the day we're going to do something about it. She opens her bag, just a crack and I can see that she's stolen Frankie's buzzer and a large pair of kitchen scissors. No way.

But this little voice in my head goes: yes way, and I get this huge adrenaline rush, and I'm like . . . fine. Okay. Let's go. So I stick my hand up as straight as I can and I ask Mr. MacLean if I can go to the bathroom. Kate grins from ear to ear. She leans forward and whispers: "Third floor."

The third-floor bathroom is practically abandoned. No one ever goes there because it smells weird. There are dirty stairs that lead to nowhere and way too many mysterious stains, but it's got what we're looking for: Privacy. I hold my breath and wait for Kate. My legs swing back and forth, back and forth, and my heart feels like it's gonna pound its way out of my chest. I try to chill. I'm sweating.

Kate's got to wait six minutes. Six minutes is how long it takes for Mr. MacLean to forget I'm in the bathroom. I look at my hair in the mirror and I think about being bald. My mom's gonna be pissed. I've never acted out before. It feels like today is the time to start. Six minutes later, Kate shows up.

She pulls the buzzer and scissors out of her bra and goes for it. Long strands of hair fall into the sink. They slither down my neck. Snip snip snip. There's a huge pile of hair around my shoes at this point and I catch sight of myself in the mirror and start giggling. Really loud. It's echoing off the toilets.

God. I look like an ALIEN.

KATE: An extremely tough alien. Like you landed on Earth to steal hearts and kick ass. We should just stop here, right? This is a look.

SAM: Ha ha, I say. So she turns the buzzer on and runs it over my scalp.

It feels so good. And when she's done we look in the mirror and I look so good. The best part though, the best part is when we get back to class twenty-five minutes later and I have no hair. I walk into class and Roger almost falls out of his chair. Kate winks at him and runs her hand over the back of my head. Mr. MacLean chokes on his coffee, but pretends like it didn't happen.

TRANSFORMANCE: A TRANSGENDER LOVE STORY WITH SONGS

TJ JABLONSKI

TJ Jablonski (he/him) is a writer living in Calgary, Alberta, Canada. TJ is a multi-instrumentalist singer-songwriter with ten indie CD releases, a published author (*truth, touch and time,* 2019), and passionate emerging playwright with three staged productions as of 2022. He is an award-winning physician, proud 2SLGBTQ+ community member, speaker, trainer, media spokesperson, and educator with many international conference, radio, television, and video credits. The playwright would like to extend a special thank you to the Alberta Playwrights Network and RBC Emerging Artist's program. TJ gives all the love in the world to Monique, his family, and all members of the trans and gender-diverse community in Alberta who took the risk in supporting this theatre arts venture. Skipping Stone Foundation—you rock!

Mack inadvertently rescues Angelica at an 2SLGBTQ+ rally. This brief encounter evolves into a tumultuous relationship. Both share a lifelong struggle with gender identity and are in the process of transitioning. Their drug-addled love story is raw and unsettling. Built with interwoven monologues, dialogue, and songs, *Transformance* challenges our universal desire to grow and be loved, to be understood and belong, to succeed and transform, or to move on.

Angelica (assigned Axel, male sex at birth) is an articulate and precocious nineteen-year-old trans feminine student.

Transformance: A Transgender Love Story with Songs was first produced by Play Between Your Thighs in Calgary on March 21, 2019. It was performed by Ryan Dickinson and Matthew Oliver van Diepen with musical performances by TJ Jablonski (vocals, keyboards, guitar, and percussion) and Justin Lanouette (vocals and bass guitar), directed by Amelia Newbert, dramaturge Gordon Pengilly, with musical direction by TJ Jablonski, set design by Amelia Newbert, lighting and sound design by Jinx, and costume design by Jason Kowalchuk. The play received production support from Fairy Tales Presentation Society, Goget'm Productions, and Skipping Stone Foundation.

✦ THE FINAL CUT? ✦

ANGELICA: In grade 8, I jerk off into a cup at school. It's after class and all the other kids have gone home. I'm staying late to do an experiment in the science lab for Miss Roberts. We have just had this sex-ed talk which titillates all the junior high students and gets me thinking.

I take a drop out of the cup with a pipette and carefully put it on a glass slide and place a tiny square cover slip over and slide it under the microscope. Even before I can focus at the lowest-power lens it is like looking out a window in a rainstorm—blurry flashes everywhere. I change to the higher-power lens and get everything into crisp focus to see sperm vibrating everywhere—exactly like the pictures that the teacher showed us. They are alive, twitching, and no matter where I move the slide there seems to be an endless number all doing the same dance.

Am I ever wrong! Not only am I a boy, I am man enough to do some real damage. The thought of this is both powerful and totally terrifying. I feel like Adam and Eve simultaneously. I grab the slide off the microscope and throw it away.

My parents say they will pay to have my sperm kept in storage. They are getting desperate. An only child threatening to have their nuts cut off at age nineteen, I'm sure they hear the bomb ticking. All I can say is, I can never be my parents. I am not cut out for being a mother. I can barely make a decision to save my own life.

From the start there should be no penis. So I stand in my bathroom and consider cutting it off. It's Sunday morning, I just met Mack a week ago. He ignites this feeling in me so strongly I can't hold back any longer.

I had wrapped dental floss tightly around the shaft of my penis a few days ago but it just dug in and hurt without doing much damage. Yesterday I had scratched at my skin with a sharp kitchen knife but I didn't have the guts to even break the skin surface.

This morning the feeling is so intense, I can taste it. Now, I am definitely going to do it. I have a straight razor that I found in my dad's drawer and I stretch out my flaccid penis.

My hands are trembling and I start to hyperventilate a bit and feel light-headed. My hands start to feel sweaty and I struggle to hold the razor as it actually starts to cut through my skin. In the first instant I don't feel a thing; I am having an out-of-body experience watching me do this to myself—strangely distant and surreal. And then suddenly I'm back in my body and feeling an intense sharp pain like someone just lit a match on my skin. It really starts spurting blood and I panic. The razor falls to the floor. I grab my penis to stop the bleeding just as I hear the door open and my mother's voice. "What are you doing?" "I'm in here, taking a leak." She mumbles an apology and quickly closes the door but, even though my back is turned to her, I think she lingers just a second longer than she has to and sees the blood and the razor. My heart really starts pounding. I sound a bit too unnerved. She knows that something very serious is going down. I hold on very tight but there is still a pool of blood on the floor. Eventually the bleeding stops but it really, really stings. I put on Band-Aids, wrapping each one tighter and tighter while trying to figure out how I am going to explain things to my mom. I'm not ready.

Blood and a razor . . . Of course! I cut myself shaving for the first time with a razor and was self-conscious that I had tried and didn't know how. I grab the razor, make a quick nick on my chin, which I barely feel at all, and put a Band-Aid over this.

I let my absolute terror masquerade as utter embarrassment as I come into the kitchen with my best performance. "I tried to shave this morning for the first time with a razor and I cut myself," pointing gingerly to my chin. She still looks sheepish about barging in on me, but I could see the sheer relief and concern of a mother as she laughs with tears in her eyes. She carefully strips off the Band-Aid, gasps a little, and quickly gets some antibiotic ointment. *God, you are so gullible.* What if she saw the real cut? What kid would do what I just did? What am I thinking; am I thinking at all?

What comes now is completely unexpected—a wave of intense adoration for my mom mixed with sheer dread. I'm ashamed by the guilt and longing for her love. A Judas kiss of betrayal for what I know I am going to do to her in the future. I have just dodged a bullet—for now.

CROOKED

SEELEY QUEST

seeley quest (sie/hir) is a trans disabled environmentalist, working in literary and body-based composition, curation, and facilitation. Sie presented in San Francisco's Bay Area from 2001 to 2014, with Sins Invalid from 2007 to 2015. Hir playscript *Crooked* is in *At the Intersection of Disability and Drama*, and hir first game narrative debuted for National AccessAbility Week 2020. Sie created the ecological assessment for the 2021 Buddies in Bad Times Theatre Rhubarb Festival, inaugurated a 2021 Quebec Writers' Federation disabled writers workshop, and a Queer Disabled Joy workshop for Studio 303's 2021 Queer Performance Camp. Hir script *Modeling* has had readings online with Realwheels Theatre, Teesri Duniya Theatre's 2020 Fireworks Program, Centaur Theatre's 2021 Wildside Festival, Vancouver's 2022 rEvolver Festival, and in person with Eastern Front Theatre's 2023 Early Stages Festival. Hir work has been published in *Canadian Theatre Review*.

Crooked is a solo show, originally autobiographical. With monologues, poetry, mime, and song, and personas including a drag queen, a clown, and an "authentic" narrator, it explores the notion of "crooked" on physical, mental, sexual, and gendered levels, and especially accepting myself as trans and disabled. *Crooked* touches on neuroqueer perception too, and on pansexuality with a gender not "opposed to" or "same as" any other gender. It engages pain flares, sex work as a tool for perceiving others encountering my body, medical stigmatization, BDSM, childhood bullying, and reveling in performativity and fluidity on stage and with language. It includes medical props; however, passages involving femme or clown drag can be performed by anyone trans. It's not a fit for cis-identified or underage actors; disabled actors are encouraged.

The primary character is "seeley"—an androgynous non-binary person in hir twenties (could be read by actors with physical and verbal dexterity aged in their 30s to 40s), with a mix of bravado, vulnerability, and playfulness.

✦✦✦

SEELEY: The first time I'm *publicly* marked as deviant I'm eleven. I'm generally well-behaved, quiet, marginal, and get many books from the school library, including one on palm reading; why should my classmate start to tease me? But there she sits, going at it just under the radar of our teacher, and I'm paralyzed in my seat. "Two, four, six eight, let's go meditate!"

In a cheerleading style: clap thighs, then clap hands together, then snap in rhythmic pattern while chanting phrase; repeat and laugh snottily.

And here I am: *(staring at her, at a loss)* I try to have my own joke by imagining her as a giant, kid-sized frog, croaking at me.

Demo croaking the numbers, "Two, four, six, eight," throaty frog-style.

But I don't know what else to do. And still without knowing, one day suddenly I'm waiting by the door for her to come out to the playground after lunch, then start trailing some yards behind her walking to gossip with a friend. I'm just gonna keep *staring* at her silently and not move closer or step back. "What are you doing?" she says, perturbed. I stare hard, silent, hold my ground, each time she stops and asks.

Demo eyes bugged, implacable intense stare.

She's taunted me relentlessly because she's *sure* I'm a meditating deviant. Now *I* initiate. I hold *her* attention. *She* doesn't know what to do, forced to face sinister power—and she starts to cry. Then she tells a teacher, and soon the assistant dean is subscribing my dad to a flurry of curative measures for me. That starts my first-year encounter with the mental health system.

Luckily, I don't tell any of them that I've known since earlier in grade school that I couldn't possibly marry! Little matter if I might desire to be with someone—I don't much know. I just deeply know I want freedom to follow my own path. Don't want to compromise my dreaming, and who could fit with me in my particularity? I fall far when I'm dreaming; sometimes wake up on the other side of the looking glass. Mom leaves Dad when I'm six, and my younger sister and me to be raised by him. So, often without babysitters, I have to spend time entertaining myself with my imagination. My folks both stay busy teaching small-city-college theatre; I take in this scene of books and performing, and early dwell in the world of storytelling. People don't always notice me, but when they do, they see I'm a southpaw who knows how to inhabit a different space. When I learn the word "sinister," I'm not scared. Its power is just something left to me, and feels familiar.

So I'm younger now, maybe seven, eight, nine or so. I do this a lot.

> *Twist limbs up, standing on one leg while the other crosses above the standing knee and tuck foot around the calf; arms together at elbows and hands twisted around to meet at palm.*

I hold it and sit this way while eating at the table, or while standing on one foot near my father as he cooks. The control feels good, a shape to contain myself within; all the parts of me are bound as tightly as possible to my core. I guess I'm nervous; being with my dad is stressful, along with other adults and uncontrollable situations. This braiding up comforts. I don't know it's yoga, it's just one more quirky thing I do; no one ever tells me to stop.

> *Then untwist while sitting in chair, and take off vest, roll sleeves.*

When I'm thirteen, folks notice my vertebrae slouching into curves. Doctor says, A brace. My dad has some scoliosis too, but mine is worse. He's educated, but doesn't trust he might know better than the doctor in considering other alternatives. My body's starting on a long, strange trip: what is he supposed to do? Even though a cousin is also recommended this and my dad's brother decides they'll try negotiating that curve without a brace, Dad says yes, and I raise no objection. I almost never do; it doesn't occur to me to complain. So doctor says get long cotton tank tops, something to wear under its mold, or else the body suffers. My skin rubs away daily in the compromising tank tops, where the armhole gap weds it and the plastic-encased rib-strap it adheres to. Brace forever stains with my body's productions—plastic, sweat, glue, salt, hair, steel mix together.

My classmates wonder about the new look. In 1990 the first *RoboCop* film is big; after the first day I wear it a boy coins "Roboneck"—it sweeps through the school. Because I help pass on the name. Who I am through junior high and high school, you challenge me to carry a mantle of ridicule with only the agency to announce it, I'll take it on and also toss you Iron Maiden sometimes too. But you'll just wince and laugh weakly, and Roboneck will stay my name for two years. Strangers think I'm retarded. Dismiss me like folks in wheelchairs, and the rest of my excellent lame, dumb, and otherwise crippled clan—I get to learn about what it's like being in this clan. To this day, when anyone tosses off something or somebody as *lame* or *retarded* and I let it slip by, part of me dies, because those folks have been the only family I've had sometimes.

Crooked will convert your children.

THE CUNNING LINGUIST

MÓNICA GARRIDO HUERTA

Mónica Garrido Huerta (she/her) is a Mexican-born, recently Canadian, Queer artist. Her short films *Diferente* and the horror-comedy *Love You to Death* premiered at the Inside Out LGBT Film Festival. Her first solo show, *The Cunning Linguist*, was created as part of the Emerging Creators Unit at Buddies in Bad Times Theatre and won the 2016 Queer Acts Festival's Audience Award. It has been adapted as an audio play for Aluna Theatre's Studio Series and is currently in development for a full stage production. She was part of the ensemble of the show *Sketch Comedy Extravaganza Eleganza*, which won a Canadian Comedy Award. Mónica is the 2018 recipient of the Queer Emerging Artist Award at Buddies in Bad Times Theatre. She is one third of the Latinx Drag King boyband "Boiband the Boyband" and has had the pleasure of working with amazing theatre companies. She is also a Taurus and wishes you the best.

The Cunning Linguist follows the story of Mónica, a Mexican, religious, sheltered but curious girl, who realizes at a young age that she is a lesbian. She believes that God (Diosito) made her this way so she could bring His message to other queer people. Accepting this mission, Mónica enthusiastically tries to spread the queer word of Diosito in Mexico. But in doing so, she learns that the place she calls home isn't too accepting of her. Feeling discouraged about her lesbian future in Mexico, Mónica asks for a sign from Diosito, and in the form of cable TV, there it was: *Degrassi: The Next Generation*. With Diosito as her unlikely sidekick, she immigrates to Toronto, where she begins to learn more about herself, freedom, and sex.

The Cunning Linguist portrays a deeply personal and honest account of a Queer woman struggling with her identity. It is also a story about the struggle to reconcile organized religion with one's own beliefs and faith. With incredible humour, compassion, and heart-wrenching moments, *The*

Cunning Linguist portrays a deeply personal and honest account of a Queer woman struggling with her identity experiencing freedom and shame. It explores the pressures of the patriarchal culture that keeps Mónica from being her true self.

✦ EL MILAGRO DE MAMÁ ✦

MÓNICA: When I was a kid every time my friends came over my mom would tell the story of when I was born . . . she would say: "You might not know this but Mónica es un milagro. Her sister came out fast, but Mónica oh no she always needs to take her time, she needs to be sure it is safe, that people are prepared for her. Mi bebe, tan tardada . . . The birth was painful and long but the real problem began when she came out."

When I was born the room where I was delivered was infected, so when they cut the umbilical cord, bad bacteria infected my blood and I became terribly ill.

The doctors told my parents I would live at best one week, or if I made it, I wouldn't live more than three years, mostly staying in the hospital. All they had left was faith and a lot of prayers.

I had my baptism in the hospital at the same time that they gave the unción de los enfermos. In a way they were trying to welcome me to a life free of sin as well as prepare me for my entrance to heaven if I died.

My parents named me Mónica, like Santa Mónica Bendita, Madre de San Agustín, the saint of married women and Christian Mothers. But most importantly, Santa Mónica is mentioned in a kids' prayer that my parents used to say with my sister and me before going to sleep . . . Santa Mónica Bendita Madre de San Agustín danos tu bendición que ya nos vamos a dormir.

After some time, it turns out that you (Diosito) God listened, and the doctor mixed the right combination of meds and I got cured, and for my mom this was a miracle.

I am a miracle, her miracle, a lesbian miracle.

Mi mamá siempre decía tu estas destinada para cosas grandes . . . she used to believe, or maybe she still does, that I will change lives . . . but what if being queer doesn't fit with the miracle . . . ?

Sometimes I wonder, what if my mom knew that the baby she was holding in her arms was literally a baby dyke. Do you think she would have prayed as hard as she did to save me?

JATRA

SANCHARI SUR

Sanchari Sur (she/they) is a PH.D. Candidate in English at Wilfrid Laurier University. Their work can be found in *The Unpublished City* (Book*hug, 2017), which was shortlisted for the Toronto Book Awards in 2018, as well as in *Arc Poetry Magazine*, *Room*, *Flare* magazine, *Daily Xtra*, *Al Jazeera*, *Joyland*, *Toronto Star*, and on the CBC. Sanchari is a recipient of a 2022 Tin House Summer Residency, 2019 Banff Residency (with Electric Literature), 2018 Lambda Literary Fellowship in fiction, and grants from Ontario Arts Council and Canada Council for the Arts. They curate Balderdash Reading Series (established January 2017), are the co-editor of *Watch Your Head: Writers and Artists Respond to the Climate Crisis* (Coach House Books, 2020), and the editor-in-chief of *The Ex-Puritan*.

The coming-of-age play follows Trishna, a genderqueer bisexual photographer (she/they) in their early twenties in Shantiniketan, West Bengal, India. They re-encounter jatra, or Bengali street/folk theatre, that still persists in areas of West Bengal. The jatra features the story of Goddess Durga and the demon Mahishasur. In the story, Durga triumphs over Mahishasur, despite his many masks. By re-encountering jatra, Trishna begins to question the many masks they need to wear in order to pass, when in reality, they don't need any of them.

Trishna is slender and short, and likes to pass as a young boy in large crowds. They are photographing the harvest fair (Poush mela) in Shantiniketan.

✦ HIDING IN PLAIN SIGHT ✦

TRISHNA: I am fascinated with jatra. Bengali street theatre. There is something immediate about the hot, bright lights. Straight men dressed as kings and queens, demons and goddesses, their slim bodies lithe in their gaudy makeup, the synthetic wigs, the flashy costumes. The way they play their female counterparts always attracts me. There is an ease in the way they slip into their roles, their temporary guises, hiding in plain sight. I often wonder how that feels, hiding in plain sight. Hiding. On purpose. And not being judged.

I saw my first jatra performance at age three. We lived in Calcutta then. When was this—1988 or '89? We lived in an apartment in south Calcutta, not far from the railway station and the slum along the rail lines. There was a jatra troupe in my neighbourhood, and they set up just a few steps from the entrance to our apartment building. The voices of the actors drifted over a loudspeaker, the lights holding fascination for me, from what I could glimpse through the bars of our balcony. I wanted to get closer, to see why there was a crowd around the glow, to see what the fuss was about.

Ma and Baba didn't think it was a place for their three-year-old.

The audience was made up of the people from the nearby slum, the maidservants from the neighbouring buildings, and the drivers who drove cars of the same people who lived in those buildings. Even the security guard of our apartment had abandoned his post for some time and joined in.

But I knew if I cried enough, I could have my way. And since I was still their only child, they let me go with our maid. "For ten minutes only," they said.

And I? I was mesmerized.

The stories played in jatras are known ones. Stories taken from Hindu mythologies. Stories of kings and queens, of gods and demons, of good vanquishing evil. The most common story is of Goddess Durga slaying the demon Mahishasur.

In the legend of Mahalaya, Mahishasur is a master of disguises. A shape-shifting demon. He uses his masks to escape each time. But he is no match for Goddess Durga. Nobody is. She strips him of his many camouflages, seeing him for who he is. It is she who finally slays him, the master impersonator.

In *Camera Lucida*, Roland Barthes writes, "There is a kind of stupefaction in seeing a familiar being dressed differently." He is looking at a photo of his mother as he writes this. In this photo, his mother is a little girl, and as he stares at the photo, time collapses for him. He realizes that his mother is both the little girl as well as the woman who recently passed away. In this collapsing of time, he is unable to reconcile himself with the woman he knew and the girl who exists in the photo. In this collapsing of time, the familiar becomes unfamiliar. In this collapsing of time, Barthes is stupefied.

I wonder if Durga too is stupefied each time she sees Mahishasur in a different disguise. How does she unmask him each time? How does she see him through her stupefactions? How does she know to slay him and him alone?

All my life I thought I wanted to play a role. Put on makeup, a costume, pass as someone I wasn't. I failed to realize I was already playing parts. The role of a woman in the body of a woman. The role of a woman who is only attracted to men. The role of a woman who can only love one person at one time.

I want to find a way to slay my inner Mahishasurs, to remove my many masks, to stop being stupefied. I am tired of hiding in plain sight.

WHEN THE ELEPHANT IN THE ROOM IS SENT OUT

SHEETALA BHAT

Sheetala Bhat (she/her) is a researcher, playwright, and theatre artist from Karnataka, India. She is Assistant Professor at York University's Department of English. She is the author of *Performing Self, Performing Gender*, published by Manipal University Press, as well as several articles. Sheetala was a writer at Indian Ensemble's First Draft: Ideas Lab in 2020. She has worked with Chintana, a grassroots theatre company, exploring the possibilities of theatre in government schools in Karnataka.

Grappling with their desire, longing, and loss, four South Indian womxn in Canada retell four Hindu mythological narratives. When the stories of the womxn in the contemporary world begin to collide with each other, so do the goddesses whose lives have now been retold and reshaped. As the goddesses seek understanding and revenge, and fight over the conflicting details of these new stories, they begin to manipulate the four human womxn. To heal and to make peace, both the goddesses and the humans are challenged to confront together questions on culture, shame, diaspora, and queerness.

Kavita is a queer woman and a first-generation South Asian immigrant in Canada. She was raised Hindu. She is twenty-nine.

✦✦✦

Night. KAVITA *is walking up and down in the living room. The room has white walls and looks grey and somber. There is a Ganesha statue in the room.* KAVITA *tries to call her mother, who does not pick up.* KAVITA *then sends voice messages on WhatsApp. In between the voice messages, there are awkward silences. The weight of her anticipation for her mother's call hangs heavily in the room.*

Voice message 1:

KAVITA: Ma, please call me back, na? I know you are awake there. Isn't it like 8 a.m. in Bangalore?

Voice message 2:

I am leaving Toronto tomorrow night. I need to know I can come home.

Voice message 3:

We need to talk . . . well . . . about the elephant in the room. Call me, okay?

Pause.

Voice message 4:

Ma, you remember Sumana auntie, right? Your friend from college? I met her the other day. And . . . she asked about you. Well, we have met several times now. I like, you know, hearing about you from her.

Voice message 5:

I can't sleep. Sandeep left. I need to leave, Ma. He wants me gone by the time he comes back. It's nice to send you voice messages. I can at least pretend like I am talking to you.

Voice message 6:

Sumana auntie is quite the storyteller, huh? She told me this strange story about Lord Ganesha. Have you heard it? I don't think so. When people hear the same story, they are bound in the same unseen thread that is tied to a tiny part of their hearts. And they know . . . they know they have heard the same story. I feel like you haven't heard this story.

Sorry. I am rambling. I just thought I would share the story with you.

So . . . once upon a time . . .

Oh never mind. It is quite silly of me. Can you just tell me I can come home?

KAVITA *stops pacing and sits down in a chair. She gathers courage and picks up the phone again.*

Voice message 7:

So, the story. You have heard the story of how Lord Ganesha got his elephant head, right? Goddess Parvati created Ganesha out of clay when her husband Lord Shiva was away. She asked him to stand guard outside when she was bathing. Shiva came home and Ganesha stopped him at the door. Outraged by this, Shiva chopped Ganesha's head off. Parvati was distraught and Shiva asked his servants to bring the head of anyone who was sleeping with their head turned north. The servants could not find anyone but a poor elephant. They brought the elephant's head and fixed it on Ganesha's neck.

In Sumana auntie's story, that whole story was made up for the world by Shiva. There was another story. A story within a story. So here it goes.

As KAVITA *tells the story, the white walls turn to bright colored sarees and the greyish atmosphere slowly becomes more colorful.*

So, when Shiva was away, and he was often away, he would sometimes forget to take Ganga with him. Ganga, the great giver, who lived in Shiva's hair, was a friend of Parvati. When Shiva was gone, Parvati and Ganga would have a wonderful time, bathing each other, combing each other's hair, draping each other with bright golden sarees, cuddling each other, and touching each other.

Parvati loves colors, softness, and long, long hair, and sweet breasts. What has Shiva got? No roundedness, no softness. He has ashes all over his body, ew! Long hair, yes. He has long hair. If Parvati made love to Shiva, it was because of this hair. To tell the truth, Parvati wasn't really fond of his unkempt hair either. It was Ganga, the beautiful river woman who lived in his hair, that Parvati loved. Ganga flowed through Parvati's limbs, caressing and washing. And Parvati floated in her, happy and carefree. Of course, Shiva thought Parvati was loving him.

It was one of those wondrous occasions. Shiva opened his tightly tied hair and Ganga floated down, and he forgot to put her back on and left the house to do his business. Parvati and Ganga got in the bath. Oh it was delicious. And so wonderful. PARVATI . . . HAD . . . THE . . . BEST . . . ORGASM. A divine orgasm, that too. What happened next? A kid was born. Neither boy nor girl. The kid was both an idea, and a living, breathing, crying child. Remember, Parvati was a goddess. She was divine. She could do whatever she wanted. She loved elephants and decided to give the child an elephant head. She wanted the kid to be nothing like Shiva. So, Ganesha was made to be soft and big. Then Parvati sent Ganesha out to play, so that she could continue enjoying the company of Ganga. To make the child feel important, she asked Ganesha to watch the door as she continued bathing.

Voice message 8:

Call me, okay? I have decided to have a child with Nirmala. You met her last time you and Dad were here, remember? I will tell you more about it when I come home.

Pause.

Ma, I am sorry Sumana auntie left India with her husband. It must have been terrifyingly lonely for you.

THE JOURNEY OF INTERSECTIONAL QUEER THEATRE

YOLANDA BONNELL

I feel like I could sit here and talk about history. There is such a rich, full history of queer theatre going all the way back, from Sappho's poems to Shakespeare on to nightclubs and bars, the covert queer plays of the 1930s to '50s, underground stories being passed along; the buildings our queer ancestors built up so our stories could have a place to live and breathe. When I think about where queer theatre has been, I can't help but think as far back as pre-contact.

In my culture (Anishinaabe-Ojibwe), and many Indigenous Nations, oral storytelling has always been an important element in communities. Our stories are medicine. It's how we passed along teachings and knowledge and our histories—migrations, battles—stories of creation, of the land. I think about my queer and/or 2 Spirit ancestors (although that's not what we would have been called at the time) creating their own versions of queer theatre.

I think it *feels* different for everyone because for each of our communities, queer theatre history *looks* different.

Oh, the intersectionality of it all!

Like everything in human-meat-sack history, it had to start somewhere and then fragment off into segregated pieces. For white folks, the pipeline of men only being allowed to perform to white women being allowed to perform is clear. While white women were finally getting their Juliet moments (or gay white men finally getting their Juliet moments, for that matter) Indigenous folks were being banned from telling any of our stories. We were being killed for telling our stories. Of course, the caveat being that no one was allowed to *talk* about how lesbionic Celia and Rosalind actually are.

I only bring up the S guy because that time of religion and puritanical culture really fucked with everything and our queer communities had to endure it for centuries to come.

So queer stories were told over the years in secret, hidden in love letters between the *dearest of friends*, in poems, in gender impersonation, in the hyperfemme sexuality of starlets and showgirls, vaudeville.

And I imagine the fear—the bravery—it took for our ancestors to do that so that we could tell our stories freely today.

Underfunded. But freely.

Underproduced. But freely.

Under-represented if you're not a gay white male.

But freely.

I said I didn't want to talk about history, but I feel like in order to talk about where we might be headed, it might be important just to mention where we're coming from. Obviously, it's a lot more nuanced than what I just wrote, but the sense of it is there.

It's different for everyone and we all move forward slowly with various barriers and privileges.

So where are we now?

I think I may have given some passive-aggressive hints back there.

We are definitely in a different place than where we started, but that doesn't mean we don't have a ways to go.

Theatre in and of itself, in the way it functions, is ableist and not sustainable. I feel like many of us, for a small period of time, hoped that it might shift and change when so many theatre institutions were called out for systemic racism and harm in 2020. The ongoing pandemic exposed capitalism in a way the world had never seen before—the theatre industry was no exception. Many artists began asking questions around hours and pay and sustainability and whose stories they were uplifting. Who was making the decisions?

But then it sort of feels like we've collectively bounced back and basically returned to the way it was before.

When I think about how the Eurocentric theatre industry was built, I am reminded that it wasn't built for us. When I say "us"—I mean specifically queer racialized folks. I mean it wasn't built for anyone who wasn't white, but the extra barriers it put up to keep the queers out, to keep the "*minorities*" out, are clear.

So how do we fit into an institution that wasn't built for us?

I think we're still trying to figure that out.

Board members of theatre institutions are predominantly white. There's this percentage idea that happens where they will pat themselves on the back for having 50 per cent diversity on their boards. But that's not the answer. It still means that 50 per cent of the board is white, while the other 50 per cent is meant to represent every other community, often including 2SLGBTQ+. This isn't representative of all theatres, but most. It's the same with core staff and front of house. And let's not even start with the lack of disability representation across the gamut.

So if the leadership and decision-makers are predominantly straight and white and able-bodied, we can see how that echoes out into programming and development and hiring.

We can see that in how the system of theatre runs. There is no time for rest or reflection. It's about tight deadlines, fitting in as much work as possible in a small amount of time, pleasing donors, go go go!

As a queer, 2S Indigenous, brown woman with disabilities, this does not work for me.

First—the stories that are held within queer bodies can often be rife with the struggle of what it means to be queer in our variety of lived experiences. Queer immigrant stories are going to be different than queer "canadian" stories. Similarly with racialized stories—there can be levels of hard truths that we're reaching that our white counterparts are not. We are often telling stories that are indicative of our actual lived experiences.

And while some of us may have training to ground ourselves while telling these stories, many do not. And we should be given space to stop or pause or reflect or talk through. We need to be given resources as we move through these stories. But institutions often won't provide that—especially when there are deadlines.

I think this is true particularly for queer and/or 2S Indigenous performers. We perform trauma for you on our own lands and we're not even given the space to move through that safely. And then we are often feeling the impacts of colonization over and over again from the institutions who are forcing us into their model and barely letting us smudge.

Second—the current theatre model does not work for queer folks with disabilities (or any folks with disabilities, really). There is no space for madness, for bodies who need extra time or extra support. It gets to a point where our storytellers may not be able to tell stories on stages anymore because the institution cannot or will not support their needs. All of this is particularly clear when we look at tech and preview weeks, longer hours, more days in the week, no space between tech and opening. Performers are just meant to launch into their run after spending hours and hours in a dark room, and sometimes still rehearsing in the afternoons. In some cases, they're doing other shows at the same time. Some bodies can't handle that and they end up getting injured or further hurting themselves. And there is already so much stigma around depression, anxiety, PTSD, other invisible disabilities—neurodivergence or even physical ones—that a performer may not be able to advocate for themselves if they need a moment as their brain or nerves are attacking them.

And look—for some people, this model works. They love it. They are fed by it.

But it doesn't work for everyone else. And that everyone else is mostly racialized, queer, disabled artists—whose stories these theatres will have no problem getting white, straight, abled bodies to play on stage. They want our stories, but they don't seem to want to make the space it takes to have us.

Obviously, this isn't the case for all theatre institutions. Some are really trying to work with communities to shift how we're holding and telling stories.

But we still have a ways to go.

I can see that the queer stories that are being told now are starting to change. Racialized, disabled queers are still underfunded, underproduced, and under-represented.

But more and more of our stories are being programmed. Mostly in indie theatre, but I think (I hope) it ripples out.

When I think ahead, all I can do is hope.

There are pockets of independent artists and collectives working differently in spaces. Working in a safer and more sustainable way. Attempting to put disability justice in theatre at the forefront. But there needs to be more support from funding bodies and institutions. I hope they begin to see how important these stories and storytellers are to the landscape of theatre on Turtle Island.

I hope for more intersectional queer stories on all platforms. I want stories about queer joy—not just our traumas. I want 2S joy. I want queer characters to just exist in stories like we do in real life. I want us to stop being the villains.

I want to see Bi/Pan love. Poly love. Ace love. Trans love. Non-binary love.

Women loving women. Healthy queer relationships. Healthy kink. Coming of age stories about queer youth. And I want to see it all in performers of various colours, culture, and body abilities and sizes.

I want our various queer communities to feel safe and not retraumatized while we tell stories.

I hope for the future that time and space is created for these types of theatre because they're so much more interesting and so much more impactful for the communities they represent.

Yolanda Bonnell (she/they) is a bi/queer Two-Spirit Anishinaabe-Ojibwe, South Asian mixed performer, playwright, and multidisciplinary creator/educator. Originally from Fort William First Nation in Thunder Bay, Ontario (Superior Robinson Treaty territory), her arts practice is now based in Tkarón:to. She is co-artistic leader of manidoons collective, that she runs with Michif (Metis) artist, Cole Alvis. In February 2020, Yolanda's four-time Dora-nominated solo show bug was remounted at Theatre Passe Muraille while the published book was shortlisted for a Governor General's Literary Award. She won the PGC Tom Hendry Drama Award for her play, My Sister's Rage *and has taught at schools like York University and Sheridan College. Yolanda proudly bases her practice in land-based creation, drawing on energy and inspiration from the earth and her ancestors.*

CHAPTER 2
TRIGGER WARNING

BOY PLAY

KAWA ADA

Kawa Ada (he/him/his) was educated at the Boston Conservatory. After being cast on Broadway, he returned to Canada where he's played leading roles at some of the most notable theatres in the country, including Mirvish, Canadian Stage, Tarragon, Factory, the Belfry, Gateway, the Grand, and several seasons at Soulpepper and the Shaw Festival. Named Toronto's Best Actor by *NOW Magazine*, he's previously won the Best Actor Toronto Theatre Critics Award and the Dora Award for Outstanding Performance in a Leading Role. His play, *The Wanderers*, is published by Playwrights Canada Press. His other plays include *The Death of Mrs. Gandhi and the Beginning of New Physics* and *Finding Islam*.

In Afghanistan, a tea house operates as a front for an ancient practice called Bacha Bazi (or Boy Play), where boys dance and sing for wealthy men. Some men take boys home and some of the boys never return. Ilhan, a former boy dancer, trains a new generation of recruits, including one he simply calls Boy. Planning to run away with Boy and raise him as his own, Ilhan's plans quickly change after Laura, a Canadian documenting the child sex trade, comes to town. Laura wants to help Boy seek asylum in Canada, which would take him away from Ilhan, the only family Boy has known. After falling in love with Laura, Ilhan must decide between a future with her or a future with Boy.

Ilhan has never thought about being with a woman until he falls in love with Laura. He has raised Boy, whom he considers to be both son and lover. Prior to this scene, Laura tells Ilhan that, though she loves him, she must leave him in order to save Boy by bringing Boy back to Canada with her. But on her last night with Ilhan, Laura begins to experience a stomach ache she believes is brought on by a new pregnancy. She tells Ilhan she has conceived his child. In this excerpt, Ilhan reveals the true cause of Laura's pain and the lengths he's willing to go to keep Boy.

✦✦✦

ILHAN gently guides LAURA to the bed.

ILHAN: Close your eyes and think of Boy, think of his smile. Lie down now, do it—it'll help your belly to think of something else. You've seen his smile, Miss Laura.

It's the same one he had as a child. That day Shah took him from the streets, brought him home, I knew I would raise him. Boy smiled at me with those crooked teeth and cheeks so plump they press his eyes shut. I felt it, that wave in my belly. You think I've felt that way with you, even once? He said, "My mother sent me to get bread. Are you the baker?" I've sent bread to his horrible mother every week since. Ten years now. But then, he was five and I . . . I knew I had to stay for him. Even if it meant working for Shah. Even when the men no longer wanted to take me home because I was getting too old, I found a way. For Boy. I start teaching—training Shah's little money-makers to dance, sing, how to take a man with ease. But Boy, he's more special than the rest. That's why I train him to be better than them—at everything. He's a star because of me. And if I'm not near him, he doesn't feel safe. That's how *I* felt with my first keeper, the Russian: he was my brother, my father. Just how Boy feels with me. And I would have stayed with the Russian all my life. But, you understand, he had these clients—some not so good.

Beat.

There was one they called Spaghetti Man. People think it was because of his beard: long, wavy, but no. They called him Spaghetti Man because the boys he rented, they would come back with their insides hanging from their holes. Like noodles. The Russian, my beloved keeper, tried to keep me out of reach as long as possible—sometimes the boys Spaghetti Man took, they didn't come back at all. But the man couldn't wait anymore.

Beat.

When it was over, I was lucky, I walked home with everything still in place—it could have been worse. If I hadn't put a bag over his head when he was inside . . . who knows. Just before I burned his body, I looked at him for a long time, looked at his deadness. He was still hard. Even in death, men are . . . relentless. Why do you think it was so easy for me? It was my life, or his, that's why. Boy is my life now, you understand? I would do much more to keep him.

Drink, drink—it'll help the burn in your belly.

Beat.

I should tell you, Spaghetti Man did give me a gift that night. He liked to play with his boys first, draw out the terror as long as he could. With me, it was my balls he found an interest in—he squeezed them slowly, until I heard a pop; he pushed them so deep inside it took two weeks for them to drop down again. Not much comes out anymore. You understand now why I never pull out with you?

He laughs.

You see, Miss Laura, all this time you've pretended to love me, I know what you wanted from me. Now you know there's very little I can give you. Only, there's much you can take away from me. I will not let you! I thought you were different, I thought you would stay, no? You, me, Boy—together.

But you come here—all of you!—you come and take what you want. When you're done, you leave us for dead—when we're no use to you anymore. My country, the whore! So leave. If that's what you want. But not with Boy.

You don't know, people die so easy here. Your soldier brothers, they understood—that's why they left. There is death with purpose. Then there is death in Afghanistan: it is without end. It has no conscience. You think I won't harm you? You think I love you too much.

Beat.

That water I gave you, do you know where it came from . . . ?

Beat.

A bag over a man's head, it doesn't take too much time, he doesn't suffer forever. But a gift in your belly from this land—perhaps from a man you thought you knew or from a bottle he handed you—they're all the same thing in Afghanistan. Every *thing*, every *person*, they all carry the same disease for your kind. Can kill you slowly, painfully. That burning in your belly will last long. You hear me, Miss Laura? Laura of Arabia. I tell you now, no one wants to be saved by you. Better to leave this country while you can.

Really, you don't look well. Should I call the doctor now?

DADDY'S ISSUES

MERLIN SIMARD

Merlin Simard (she/they/iel/elle) is a performer, playwright, dramaturge, and filmmaker originally from Tiohtià:ke (Montréal) now based in Tkarón:to (Toronto). Her practice focuses on themes of access, gender euphoria, technology, and multilingual performance. As a performer, Merlin has worked with Factory Theatre, Crow's, Outside the March, Buddies in Bad Times, the Stratford Festival, Toronto Dance Theatre, Théâtre Français de Toronto, and many other theatre companies across Turtle Island. They co-founded and co-run bigT, a theatre collective seeking to uplift intersectional trans voices (@bigtcollective) and is currently Playwrights Unit Facilitator at the Paprika Festival. She is developing several theatre, VR, and television projects. Find more at merlinsimard.com and @hussy4hussy.

Daddy's Issues is a sixty-minute bilingual (Français/English) play that explores grief's meaning when it comes to a parent still alive. One foot stuck in her upbringing and the other one in her dad's old busted iPhone 4, Anaïs will have to mend the ruptures of her childhood to finally feel whole. This play is a love letter to those who chose to stay, the complexity of modern parenthood, the precious joy of trans women and transfemmes, and, most importantly, it is a love letter to the fractures of too-short childhoods.

Anaïs (she/her/elle) is a queer trans woman in her mid to late twenties who lives in Tiohtià:ke. One stubborn bitch, she isn't scared to argue herself to death in English or in French.

✦✦✦

ANAÏS: Quand t'était partie j'ai eue un rêve que j'étais enceinte.

LETTY: You took a nap?

ANAÏS: Non.

Mon ventre était tellement immense, mais not like a miracle of life kind of way, mais genre plus dégeu. And everyone was acting like this was the most normal thing ever. Genre, dans le rêve, ma mère était même venue avec des vêtements de bébé à moment donné.

BUT it was like I knew that I was trans, and I didn't have a vagina—um sorry—uterus, but the rest of the world didn't. Puis j'tais comme, you know "what the fuck, how am I fucking pregnant?"

> *LETTY laughs. / LETTY rit.*

Puis là, plus tard dans le rêve, genre fast forward ou de quoi de même, I was giving birth pi quand le bébé est sorti y ressemblait à deux gouttes d'eau à mon père. But like back at the age when I last saw him, just before he disappeared. And it was fucking weird parce que y'était en train de crier, encore genre mouillé du genre de fluide de vagin. And like he said that he knew that I wasn't supposed to be pregnant, that I was a glitch in the universe. And he, like, started wailing, in the shrill way newborn babies do, you know? And then he said:

(wailing like a baby / gémissant comme un bébé) Tu vas toujours être mon tit gars.

Puis là, je sais pas de où j'ai pogné mon courage, mais je lui ai dit:

C'est toi le tit gars. Tu l'as toujours été.

And then, I just woke up. But like *what*. C'est pas whack de rêvé d'accoucher son père?

And I've just been thinking about *children* et que *si jamais* je changeait d'avis, comment je l'éduquerais. Avec tellement de soin, d'honnêteté et de patience que j'ai pas encore.

And then I also got worried that if I was so focused on not raising children the way that I was raised, de m'en allé le plus loin possible de mon enfance que j'pouvais, j'reviendrais juste à la même place.

Walking around the earth, straight back into my dad's grasp.

Ce que j'ai plus envie, on dirait, c'est de retourner sur me pas. Retourné vers moi même, en fait. À la personne qui existait avant que la fiction devienne vérité.

FUTURISTIC JOURNEY THROUGH THE PUSSY PORTAL

JENNIFER MURRIN

Jennifer Alicia Murrin (she/they) is a queer, mixed Mi'kmaw and settler (German/Irish/Scottish) multidisciplinary artist originally from Elmastukwek, Ktaqmkuk (Bay of Islands, Newfoundland), now residing in Toronto. She is a two-time national poetry slam champion and collective member of the Toronto Poetry Project and Seeds & Stardust. Her work has been featured in *Canthius Magazine*, NOW *Magazine*, on the CBC, and at the imagineNATIVE Film + Media Arts Festival. Jennifer Alicia co-edited the Indigenous poetry anthology *The Condor and the Eagle Meet* and has a debut chapbook titled *Mixed Emotions*. She is a current participant in the Animikiig Creators Unit through Native Earth Performing Arts, working on her debut play, *To Go Home*. Find out more about her work at jenniferalicia.com.

✦✦✦

A queer Indigenous futuristic journey
Beginning with, my pussy

The pulse in my lips vibrating like the Big Drum
I call you into Grand Entry
Our movements in sync like moontime
Rippling tides growing as we dance
Ceremony is commencing and you're about to be healed

Let my waters erupt
Nourish you
Water is life
Sounds like the cones on my Jingle Dress when sidestepping
Like rain on tin roofs

I feel the power like an honour beat at the pow wow
Sends us exploding into the cosmos riding a shooting star
Sexed so good that it transcends time and space
Time immemorial
It is the past, now, and future all at once

Time immemorial because the place we land in the galaxy is before the
  beginning
We are the ancestors now of a future imaginary that has already passed
My pussy, be the portal
We, be the time travellers
We are now on NDN time transcending into the cosmos
We are celestial beings
Returning to the stars as star people
Returning to ourselves in the future
I welcome you to the queer Indigenous future

Here, we resist colonial gender binaries
Here, our culture is in continuous orbit
Here, our stories and songs in our languages vibrate through frequencies transmitting cultural knowledge
Here, Indigiqueers run shit

On this planet in the future, Indigenous women and Two-Spirit peoples use their love and rage to transform communities
As we have ALWAYS been the backbone, but no longer breaking our backs
We have revitalized our ceremonies
We have recognized our gifts
We have remembered our roles

Our past and current trauma cleansed by smudge released from craters in the soil
Our medicines grow free from capitalism
Our culture be the electromagnetic force that brings cluster star communities together
Our dances, so powerful that they produce asteroids ridding our planet of the unwanted
Our dreams are the manifestation of reality
The same way our ancestors dreamt of this present world for us
We aspire to be good ancestors in the future

An Indigenous queer future is not difficult to imagine when it is already written in our birth charts
Mapped out by our ancestors in the constellations
Tangible through the supernova star that exists within my pussy
When it combusts, we are taken to another dimension where we bask in the afterglow of the nebula

See dawn on the horizon
Dawn, the first light of a new day, ending of night
Where the past and future come together in the now
Welcome to the queer Indigenous future

SWEET-TALK

MATTHEW WINTER

A gay/queer, able-bodied second-generation Canadian settler of Chinese, Filipino, Hispanic, and British heritage whose writing is inspired by Brecht and the qualities of post-dramatic storytelling, Matthew Winter (he/they) is interested in writing work that excites an actor, innovates the form, and impacts an audience. Born and raised in so-called "Vancouver, BC," Matthew has devised and performed in multiple works during his time at Simon Fraser University's School for the Contemporary Arts, and with theatrecorps, the company Matthew co-founded. Currently, Matthew's time is spent working in production at a VFX studio, watching the most recent episodes of *The Real Housewives*, and daydreaming about food. When able, he hopes to continue creating for the theatre.

Sweet-Talk is a dark comedy that takes place at the home of Aphrodite and Ares on their wedding anniversary. The drama begins to unfold when Psyche rejects Eros's love, causing him to become an emotional mess, resulting in a chain of events that either unravel this lavish affair or make it even more exciting. *Sweet-Talk* is vulgar, haughty, and incredibly dramatic.

Pothos (they/them, Greek, 1,000,000,040 years old, immortal, able-bodied, gender nonconformist, pansexual, polyamorous) is the god of sexual longing, yearning, and desire. They encourage mortals to act upon their desires. They enjoy drama and conflict, and live for lust. Though, when it comes to appeasing their mother, Aphrodite, Pothos bends over backwards.

✦✦✦

POTHOS: She called me, and told me to get her son, and I said yes without hesitation. I am here, and you are behaving like a sad boy again—so damn fragile. Staring in the mirror? I see perfection. You don't think you're perfect? You're a fucking God—God of love and sex—staring into a mirror made with mortal hands. Let me pick you up from the ground and tell you, you rival the perfection that the homosexual only wishes it had. Don't be offended that I compared you to a mortal term—bear with me. It's at the forefront of my mind. I can kill three birds with one stone: express this thought, lift your spirits, and aid our mother. Mortals. They love to party. They love to dance. I watch them from a bird's-eye view. It's like I'm watching that reality show, *Too Hot to Handle*—I just finished the new season. My mind goes numb, I lose track of time, all my responsibilities fall to the wayside, and I lose my sense of purpose. I see thousands stepping into the tradition of marriage, to just fall apart because they've committed to edging the same phallus for decades! What's that saying Eros? The saying with the pegs? You can't fit a circle square . . . you can't fit a square block into a circle. Is that a peg? Stop crying. Psyche breaking your heart is the least of your worries. You will heal from this rejection—you are made of pure energy—you're fine. The homosexual has their strengths, but some of them carry *many* flaws; they're not as "oppressed" as they thought they once were. The ones that are steeped in wealth and riches whine, and whine, and whine. Whining! It's sexy sometimes. I met this mortal whose calves were as chiselled as Hercules, with thighs as thick as Achilles. So supple that I thought I died, but that's impossible. Just shows you how much of a pervert I am in mortal form! Legs! I crumble for legs. If legs were Ox shit, I would be obliterated by them. When their cloths lift high enough to preview a pair of toned vastus medialis and/or vastus lateralis, I cum on the spot. It's odd how vulgar I'm being— It's like I *am* a homosexual. You're not listening, are you? I'm depicting how rich the homosexual experience is, in hopes for you to realize that maybe going after a phallus, then a vagina, may be more rewarding for you? What drives you,

Eros? Femininity? Masculinity? A mixture of both? None? What drives you, Eros? Psyche?! Does Psyche really bring out something in you that no other fucking being, or non-being, does? A God experiencing mortal drama can be such a nuisance, but because I love you, I shall not label it as such. Listen, and listen to me closely, on my way here I was swept off my feet by a thick-legged mortal. What captivated me was his legs and not his phallus! How hetero of me. Do I make everything, and everyone, desire me if I walk past them, yes, but I felt like this interaction was very genuine. We tore into each other's flesh like it was forbidden fruit, and we indulged in positions that even *you* would find incredible. Did I sweat? No. Did he die? Maybe. My irreverence towards mortals does waver—you know this. Stop pouting! Don't my escapades excite you? Make you smile? Or do they make you yearn for what you don't have? To be honest, I'm getting tired of you wanting what's not yours in the first place. Yes, we are Gods, but please don't become like Zeus. That gross piece of shit. At least Mother has taste and never went for that misogynist. Though, the one she is with now is cut from the same crusty, mouldy, rotten cloth: Adonis. Speaking my own thoughts is making me *very* tired, and I no longer want to. Take my kiss, take your smooth ass, and go speak to Mother. She wants to know why you're causing drama, and she wants it to end. Love you.

GRAPE HEAD

EISH VAN WIEREN

Eish Van Wieren (they/them) is a white (Dutch/UK) trans non-binary trans-disciplinary theatre practitioner, performer, playwright, mask maker, and costume designer originally from Mohkinstsis/Calgary and currently based in Tkarón:to/Toronto. They also work in film and TV. Eish is passionate about staging diverse queer/trans stories and building production teams that reflect/support the stories being told on stage while working in an anti-oppressive framework. They hold an M.F.A. in Performance Creation, were a member of Playwrights' Workshop Montréal Young Creator's Unit 2021 to 2022, Tarragon Theatre's extended Young Playwrights Unit 2021, the Nightwood Innovators 2022 to 2023, and Factory Theatre's Training Enhancement Program. You can find them on Instagram @splatbonfitz_productions.

Grape Head is a mask-based theatrical work that tells the story of Ampelos, a genderfluid trans/non-binary bi/pansexual, obsessed with fermentation and Dionysus, who discovers they are metamorphosing into a grape. With the world as they knew it changed, Ampelos must navigate their chaotic fall into self-understanding through queer transformation, all while making a vat of wine to offer to Dionysus. *Grape Head* is coming out story, meets Kafka's *The Metamorphosis*, meets a reversed version of *The Bacchae*. Dionysus is reimagined as Gox, a non-binary trans entity that Ampelos worships, loves, and becomes, as self becomes lover becomes deity. Using poetic language and vivid imagery, *Grape Head* explores things in life and nature that, though not seen with the eye, are revealed to have always been there.

Grape Head was first produced by Splatbonfitz Productions at York University, Toronto, on May 21, 2021. It was performed by Eish Van Wieren, directed and dramaturged by Jay Northcott, with sound design and editing by Sam Page. It was workshopped in December 2022 at Playwrights' Workshop Montréal with support from the Canada Council for the Arts. It was directed by Murdoch Schon, with dramaturgy by Jesse Thomas Stong, and performed by Lior Maharjan and Erin Lindsay.

✦✦✦

AMPELOS bikes down the road. They have to avoid things that you might find on the Toronto streets. They are a grape out in the world.

AMPELOS: Dionysus was the most popular kid in their class;
however not really because they liked to get into trouble.
Liked to arrive late.

I liked to arrive late, so when I met them on the danforth, outside of the ttc, outside of time,
both of us blew smoke through mouths;
through each other's mouths,
and into the pits of our stomachs.

A couple of lesbian gay bisexual theybies out on the street,
inside of the moonlight;
always outside until inside.
Bits and parts.
Inside, outside.
Outside, inside.
Fleshy bits.
Gushy bits.
Softy bits.
Chunky bits.
Of skin, of amethyst, of blood, of violets, of bones, of forests.

Beat.

So they took me home, but it was my home, so really I took them home,
and we lost track of which one of us was which.
Both of us losing ourselves: but them never having a self in the first place.

Earlier that night I bought them a cocktail from a fancy cocktail bar,
but they poured it out and climbed behind the bar to grab a bottle of red,
from some region in spain, some region in the east of spain,
that they had ordered once, that they had made once,
that someone had poured for them once.

From flesh.
My flesh.
Poured the wine from spain out of my flesh and into their glass.
Then we were out on the danforth, out in the cold,
a night ride on a streetcar going south and then west on queen.

Beat.

Sometimes they say the wrong thing to me and it makes me laugh.
Sometimes they say the wrong thing to me and it makes me cry.
But we always arrive at the same place: the middle of nowhere.
Licking each other's ins, licking each other's outs,
and whispering melodic sighs by each other's ears.

They are me until they're not.
I am them until I'm not.

Beat.

As a teen, Dionysus had a hand-carved thyrsus that they used to smash mailboxes.
Hated the anticipation of waiting for mail to arrive.
"It will come when it comes and leave when it leaves.
I don't want to think about it till it's there."

Beat.

We met at strip club at lansdowne and bloor, a block east of lansdowne and bloor,
there were beautiful dancers performing years of hard work.
Masters of their craft.
One dancer worth a thousand business suits on bay street.

A box of wine, three muff dives, and a melodic sigh later,
we're out the door and on the way to my house.
Only I was alone with them inside my belly: a drink inside my belly.

They come from the sky, stitched inside of lightning.
Or that's what they told me.
Really they're from alberta too.
East west in calgary on crowchild trail,
a block or two from 17th ave,
on the alley parallel to center street.

Before I knew them, I knew them.
Inside. Outside.
Outside. Inside.

People can get over anything.
Anything can get over people.
However they are not people and I am not anything.
Just fluid.
Fluids.
Two fluids.
Fluidy.
Anything but over and over but anything.

TAB & LANDON

JAY WHITEHEAD

Jay Whitehead (he/they) is the creator or co-creator of shows including *UNSEX'd*, *Tab & Landon*, *333*, and *Castrati—An Electro Drag Opera*. For Theatre Outré Jay has appeared in and/or directed productions including *Montparnasse*, *A Streetcar Named Desire*, *The Curing Room*, *The Confession of Jeffrey Dahmer*, *How to Leave*, *Late Company*, *Like Orpheus*, and *My Funny Valentine*. He has worked as an actor, director, choreographer, and teacher in cities across Canada and abroad. He is the recipient of the Micheál Mac Liammóir Award for acting and the Hilton Edwards Award for directing at the International Dublin Gay Theatre Festival in Dublin, Ireland. Whitehead is a former artistic director and co-founder of Theatre Outré, a queer mandated theatre company operating out of Lethbridge, Alberta, which will celebrate its tenth season in 2022/2023.

A graphic reimagining of the Old Testament story of Cain and Abel set against the backdrop of 1970s smut, *Tab & Landon* graphically explores the complicated and incestuous relationship between twin brothers: the charismatic and athletic Landon and his sensitive and possessive brother Tab. To make ends meet, having lost their father to a prolonged illness, they turn to the world of pornography where they perform together in "twincest flicks;" but the lines begin to blur between the onscreen fantasies they create and their real-life relationship as it begins to unravel with murderous results. *Tab & Landon* is a salacious parable that explores themes of family, lust, and revenge of biblical proportions.

Tab, a sensitive and naive young man who confuses sex with love, and who is also infatuated with his twin brother, Landon, confides in "Man," a pornography director who gets off on digging into the personal life details of his performers. Tab reveals a shocking secret about his relationship to his dying father.

Tab & Landon was first produced by Theatre Outré, Lethbridge, on April 20, 2017. It was performed by Allister MacDonald, Brett Dahl, and Jay Whitehead; directed by Jay Whitehead; with sound design by Katharine Zaborsky; set, costume, and lighting design by Deonie Hudson; and projections and videography by Lyndsay Labrecque.

✦✦✦

TAB: I took care of Dad at the end, that's it. Mom obviously couldn't. Landon was busy with sports and an actual social life. So, yeah, I guess Dad did come to rely on me in the end even if it wasn't by choice.

I did what I felt was right, ok? Someone had to be there for him. He was in such a haze of painkillers, I doubt he even knew I was there anyways. And this one night, I was just sitting at his bedside reading, and Dad makes this noise. But not a sick noise. It was a sexy noise. Like this low moan, you know, like he was having this kind of sex dream or something. When I looked up, he seemed peaceful enough. But under the sheets I could see it popped up as plainly as anything. It was practically lifting the sheets off of him. I didn't even think he could still get hard in his condition. It was impossible not to see it, though. And I started wondering if his looked the same as mine, you know. I think I was just looking for proof that I was his son. That if our bodies looked somehow similar, I'd feel comforted in my relationship to him. So, I moved in closer. He was dead to the world, right out of it. I lifted the sheets, gingerly, quietly back to see. I held my breath. Lifting, looking, fearing. And there it was poking right out of the fly of his jockey shorts. And I just stared at it. Blank. It was so fucking ugly. Just this vile-looking thing. Hairy, waxy, bright red almost. Just alien looking. I was staring and staring at this grotesque cock. My father's cock. And it was so ugly it was hypnotizing. I was frozen. And Dad suddenly makes this snorting noise which broke me out of whatever trance I was in. And when I looked at his face he was staring right into my eyes. But, like, right into them. And he was completely lucid. More lucid than I'd seen him in weeks. And the look he was giving me, oh, I recognized that look from all the fly balls I'd ever dropped, or C minuses I'd ever gotten in wood shop, or beds I'd ever wet at three in morning. That familiar look of profound disappointment and disgust. And we stayed like that. And he bore into me with that look. And then he finally cracked open his pasty, rancid, sick mouth as if to speak. It seemed as if he tried to force the words out for hours. And then, when he did, all he could manage to croak out of his dusty throat was one word. One fucking word.

"Queer!"

And all those dropped balls and C minuses and wet beds passed silently between our eyes one final devastating time. But inside I knew that this time at least, I had the upper hand. So, I looked back down at that gargoyle of a penis: my own throbbing genesis pointing accusingly back at my flushing face. I held him down with my arms, he was too weak and too drugged-up to resist at all. It was just too easy. And then I showed him just how queer his son really was. And I made sure he enjoyed it too. If I was going to hell for being queer, then I'd make goddamn sure he was going there first. Then I put the pillow back under his head, I cleaned him up, I tucked him in, and I went to bed.

Look, I don't regret it and I'm not ashamed. I'm nobody's victim. Mom found him dead the next morning.

CHAPTER 3
WHEREVER YOU ARE

THE BEAVER

JOHNNIE McNAMARA WALKER

Johnnie McNamara Walker (he/they) is a queer writer and performer best known for his solo show *Redheaded Stepchild*, which has toured Canada coast to coast. His newest solo show, *Iggy Beamish*, debuted at the Edmonton Fringe Festival in 2023 and his previous solo show, *The Heterosexuals*, has been performed in Toronto, Edmonton, and Dublin. His play *Shove It Down My Throat* premiered at Buddies in Bad Times Theatre in 2019. He has held residencies at Buddies, Canadian Stage, Theatre Passe Muraille, Videofag, and Playwrights' Workshop Montréal. His short film *Saturn Devours* has appeared at film festivals in Toronto, Los Angeles, and Montréal. He is a founding member of queer burlesque troupe BoylesqueTO and has hosted dozens of their shows. Johnnie is also a DJ and the creator of long-running queer nightlife series HEY GIRL HEY.

This piece first existed as a Facebook post, written as a kind of eulogy for the best queer bar Toronto ever had. The version printed in these pages reimagines it as a short solo performance/seance in which The Beaver is revived one last time—in our imaginations, at least.

The Beaver (2006 to 2020) was a Queen West institution: a beloved queer bar and cultural hub founded by Lynn MacNeil and Will Munro (a hugely influential artist and event promoter who died way too young). Countless DJs, drag performers, and musicians cut their teeth doing gigs at The Beaver. It was also the site of innumerable breakups, make-outs, karaoke meltdowns, bathroom blowjobs, first kisses, last dances, and glorious performance art catastrophes. The pandemic caused The Beaver to close her doors for good, leaving Toronto's entire Queer West End scene heartbroken. Johnnie the character is the same person as Johnnie the author: a gorgeous thirty-something writer/performer who still misses that dingy little dive bar near Queen and Gladstone.

✦✦✦

Darkness. Then, a spotlight illuminates a solitary figure: JOHNNIE.

JOHNNIE: You wait.

A pause.

And you wait. And you wait and you wait and you wait and you wait and you wait and you wait and you wait until it's the year 2006 and you are twenty-one years old. And now, here you are on Church Street. Because everyone knows Gay means Church Street. And you are finally ready . . . to wait just a little bit longer.

You linger outside the door to one of Those Bars, thrilled and terrified by the certainty that you're about to meet The Rest Of Your Life. What will you find on the other side of that door? Sex? Love? The home planet you've been zipping around the galaxy in search of for as long as you've been alive? These things could all be right here, behind this door. And *more*! Things you've never even dreamed of, things your body doesn't even know it needs yet. And all you have to do is take a deep breath and . . . Open. That. Door.

But . . .

You do not find those things behind that door. Or the next one. Or the one after that.

You think: this can't be *it*, can it? There's got to be another door I haven't tried.

You don't have any Gay friends yet to ask for advice, but a sympathetic Hetero pal takes pity on you and reaches out, on your behalf, to the

LiveJournal community. (Remember: it's 2006.) And that's when you first hear that name; a dirty joke murmured down a digital game of broken telephone:

The Beaver.

> *Slowly, the lights begin to fade up, revealing an endearingly grubby dive bar. Old half-torn event posters taped and thumbtacked to the red walls, a scuffed-up checkerboard tile floor, a Tom of Finland mural peeking out from the corner . . .*

You walk further west on Queen Street than you've ever walked before. Years later, the neighbourhood's seediness will be scrubbed clean, but right now, it still gives off a whiff of filth and danger. Abell Street is dotted with ramshackle artist lofts instead of condos. CAMH retains the foreboding walls of its Provincial-Lunatic-Asylum past, each brick laid by the patients themselves. You don't linger outside the door this time.

Later, you will find out The Beaver only opened earlier this year, but there's nothing about the dive bar that feels brand new, and the names you hear whispered in connection to it . . .

> *An audio track fades up, giving us the faint din of bar conversation, through which we can just make out: "Will Munro . . . Vazaleen . . . "*

. . . they feel like long-kept secrets you've only just been let in on.

> JOHNNIE *walks to one side of the stage, where the hand of an unseen person passes him a drink in a highball glass. He takes a sip.*

You shuffle over to the bar and order something absolutely embarrassing only to be starstruck when your Long Island Iced Tea is handed to you by Reg, whom you recognize from magazine covers and the latest John Cameron Mitchell film.

And maybe you don't fall in love that night. Maybe you don't have sex. Maybe you just finish your drink, say goodbye to Reg, and walk home. But when you do, there's a smile on your face because just maybe—for the first time in your life—you've touched down on a planet that felt like home.

Of course you come back. For drinks. For brunch. For dinner. For dancing. For drag. For karaoke. For the *patio*! Sometimes just to see who's in tonight. Your first real date is at The Beaver. It's pretty bad! Your first DJ gig is at The Beaver.

> *Coloured "party lights" flash and rotate. We can just barely make out an up-tempo song by Peaches or the Hidden Cameras playing in the background.*

It's also pretty bad, but both are activities you'll improve at with a little practice.

> *The music gets louder.* JOHNNIE *has to raise his voice to talk over it.*

Time passes. The lofts come down. The condos go up. You watch a constellation of other West End queer bars light up: Naco, The Henhouse, The Steady, Holy Oak, Less Bar. And, one by one, you watch them burn out again. But your north star on Queen West somehow endures. And you hear the rumours: "*her days are numbered . . . the writing's on the wall . . .* " But when you look at the wall, all you see are Lee's and Eric's murals which, even when they're brand new, like The Beaver herself, feel like they've been there forever. Like they'll *be* there forever.

> *On the back wall, a large canvas unfurls. It's Will Munro's iconic Beaver Flag: a white background containing the black outline of a beaver, bisected by three lightning bolts—one pink, one blue, one yellow.*

You come back.

And you come back. And you come back and you come back and you come back until it's March 13, 2020, and it's your birthday and you've just turned thirty-five and nobody knows it yet, but it's the last night she'll ever be open. You wear low heels, a Value Village bustier, smeared azure eyeshadow, and a deceptively glamorous cheap wig. On Friday nights, you DJ a *Drag Race* viewing party just down the street and you always come here after.

But tonight is Different. Something in the air. Like petrichor, that earthy smell before the rain. (Only 10 per cent of people can smell petrichor. You can.) All night long your phone buzzes with texts from friends: *sorry, just feel weird about coming out tonight!* (Months later, the same friends will text you again: *can't believe I missed the last night to have fun before the world ended!*) But you don't want it to be Different. You grab a rye and ginger and hit the postage-stamp tiny dance floor, sweating your makeup off to Robyn and Kylie Minogue. Was there a queer bar on Krypton? What was it called? What music was the DJ playing the night it all went kaboom?

> *The music crescendos.* JOHNNIE *dances, downing his drink. The music fades. The party lights go out. We return to the tight spotlight from the beginning.*

At the end of the night, before you walk out the door for the last time, you linger for a moment. You look back. You wave goodbye. And you turn to your husband and say: "I guess it'll be a little while before we're back here again."

> *Fade to black.*

OUT IN/OF COMMUNITY

CHARLIE PETERS

Charlie Peters (ze/hir/hirs) is a proudly queer theatre and opera director, performer, creator, lighting designer, dramaturg, playwright, poet, and clown. Born, raised, and continuing to live on Treaty 6 Territory and the homeland of the Metis Nation, hir family traces its roots back to England, Poland, and the Campbell lands of Scotland. Hir artistic work has been seen on stages (and in parks, fields, school gyms, living rooms, and swimming pools) across Western Canada. Hir degrees include a B.F.A. in acting from the University of Saskatchewan as well as an M.F.A. in theatre practice and an M.A. in gender and social justice studies from the University of Alberta. Ze trained extensively at the Manitoulin Conservatory for Creation and Performance and currently serves as secretary of the Saskatchewan Association of Theatre Professionals. Ze is folk trail and live theatre coordinator at the Silver Skate Festival, founding director of Embrace Theatre, and a former artistic associate with Sum Theatre. Hir scholarly work has been published in *Theatre Research in Canada*, *Canadian Theatre Review*, *Comedy Studies*, *Canadian Theatre Encyclopedia*, and on *HowlRound*. Visit www.charliepeters.ca for more information.

A chorus speaking poetry guides the audience back and forth between storylines and timelines, giving literal voice to the queer community. Five sets of characters intersect and diverge. This work-in-progress play explores queerness through the interwoven lives and storylines of a variety of queers wrestling with their various responses to the protests and social reckonings sweeping their communities.

Jim is a white cis man in his fifties. He is a veteran of the clubs, a survivor of the AIDS epidemic, and has become fiercely apolitical since meeting his husband. Several years ago he befriended Jane, a woman in her late twenties. He says he loves her like a sister. He just doesn't believe she's queer.

But Jane also harbours strong feelings about Jim's queerness: he and his husband work in a bank, have a literal picket fence around their house, and refused to attend the protest she was just arrested at. She may be marrying a man, but it is Jim who stands for everything status quo. As far as she's concerned, Jim may be gay but he isn't queer.

✦ JIM TELLS JANE HOW IT IS ✦

JIM: Okay I just have to say it
This has been a long time coming
And I'm not trying to be prejudiced or whatever
I'm really not
I'm just telling it like it is
A little hard truth for you tonight

You are not

Queer

You're not queer
I'm sorry but it's true
You live with a man
You're marrying him
I mean my god girl
You're planning to wear white at the wedding and have your dad give you away
I know I know
Your mom too
Escorting you down the aisle
As a gross hetero couple
You're a feminist
I know I know
But like
The wedding's going to be at the legion in your hometown
The
Legion
You can't have a gay wedding at the legion in fucking nowhere Saskatchewan

Look
This bisexual thing
I don't care who you made out with in college
Or slept with even
I don't care what porn you watch
Or if everybody in the whole world turns you on
You're marrying a man honey
You
Are not

Queer

Don't get upset
I'm not mad
I'm really not
But somebody has to tell you
Tell it like it is
Because you're watering it down for the rest of us

You didn't
You DON'T
None of you suffer for it like we did

Posting a rainbow flag to your profile
While you're still dating Mr. Chiselled Jaw
That's not what coming out is like
Not for us
Not for real queers
That's being straight and wanting attention
Or wanting to get laid
I don't even know what it is
But it ain't queer
So it's straight
It's actually straight

Drunk chicks making out at the club and staring at the queens like it's a fucking zoo then going home to gay-bashing boyfriends and letting them fuck you in the ass which is fine because you have a vagina but when we do it we're fucking faggots who need to be taught a lesson

Not Jamal
I know
He's sweet
You know I like him
But he's not gay
He's not queer
And neither are you my dear
So you need to fuck right off with that "I'm queer too" bullshit
Just fuck right off

I'm sorry

I love you like a sister
I really do
But you're not actually queer

I'm telling you honey
You're not

AGOKWE

WAAWAATE FOBISTER

Waawaate Fobister (he/him) is an actor, dancer, playwright, choreographer, producer, and a Grass Dancer. Waawaate means Northern Lights, and he is a proud Anishinaabe from Grassy Narrows First Nation. He's a recipient of the Dora Mavor Moore Award for Outstanding Performance and New Play for *Agokwe* (in total, the play received six awards), the Humber College Outstanding Actor Award, and the Mark S. Bonham Centre Award from the University of Toronto. He also has many nominations, including the Ontario Premiers' Award, the K.M. Hunter Award, and the Sterling Award—Edmonton. He trained and studied at Humber College, the Banff Centre for the Arts, Summer School of Toronto Dance Theatre, and completed intensives at the Centre for Indigenous Theatre and Kaha:wi Dance Theatre. Waawaate has worked for many major theatre companies across Canada. His work has taken him to many places as an artist, including Japan, the UK, and many coasts across Turtle Island. He was also a playwright-in-residence at Native Earth and Magnus Theatre.

Agokwe explores unrequited love between teenage boys from neighbouring reserves. Mike is a hockey player and Jake is a traditional dancer. The boys notice each other at the Kenora Shoppers Mall and ultimately connect through a mutual love of movement. They meet briefly at a post-hockey-tournament 49er, where they bashfully confess their desire for each other. But youth, distance, and isolation strive to pull the threads apart.

Agokwe was first produced by Buddies in Bad Times Theatre, Toronto, on September 23, 2008. It was performed by Waawaate Fobister, directed by Ed Roy, with music by Marc Nadjiwan, lighting design by Kimberly Purtell, set design by Andy Moro, costume design by Erika Isteroff, sound design by Lyon Smith, and stage management by Tracy Lynne Cann.

✦✦✦

JAKE: The first time I saw Mike was at the Kenora Shoppers Mall. I remember it like it was yesterday. I had driven into town to buy a new pair of jeans. I was mindin' my own business, making my way to the Warehouse One jeans store, when suddenly I got this creepy feeling that someone was watching me. You know that feeling when the hairs on the back of your neck stand on end? I slowly did a glaze-over of the mall and there he was standing opposite of Warehouse One; the most beautiful Ojibwe boy I have ever seen was staring at me and I couldn't help but stare back. He's nice and tall. He had nice, dark, glowing Indian skin. Nice toned-muscle arms. Nice developed chest. Nice hair. Nice eyes. Nice lips. Oooo . . . Nice basket. Just sooooooooooooo nice . . . hmm. It felt like we were staring at each other for eternity, even though I am sure it was only for a few seconds, but in that brief time the heat between us had become so intense I had to look away. When I gathered my courage to look back, he was gone. In that moment I had these emotions, feelings, sensations I had never felt before. Was it love or lust at first sight? I didn't know and I didn't care. All I knew was I had to know everything I could about him. I couldn't tell anybody why. I am not even sure I knew myself. So, I described him to Goose and asked if she knew him, and she did. Of course, she also wanted to know why I was asking about him. I made up some lie that he stole some girl that I was trying to pick up. Although she was pissed off hearing about this, she told me his name was Mike. Oh . . . Mike. Mike. Mike. Because of the hockey tournament this weekend there is going to be a lot of parties and huge lineups to get in the bars. I am not really quite old enough, but I have a fake ID. My cousin Goose made me a fake Indian Status Card. It better freakin' work because some assholes don't take status cards. But that doesn't matter. I just can't wait. There are pretty much three bars in Kenora. There is the ghetto Native bar where all the old stinky Natives go . . . and now that I think of it there are some old stinky white people that go there too. Then there is this cool young hip white bar where all the cool whiteys go, which I probably won't go to just because I am not really white enough. That means I am going to go to Milltown, the cool Native bar. There ain't no question in my mind that's where I'm going to go because that's probably the bar where Mike is going to be. *(fearful and excited)* Eeeeeeeeeeeeeeeeee . . .

FALLING IN TIME

C.E. GATCHALIAN

Born and raised on the unceded territories of the Musqueam, Squamish, and Tsleil-Waututh peoples (colonially known as Vancouver), now based primarily in Tkarón:to (Toronto), C.E. Gatchalian (he/him/his) is a Filipinx diasporic queer author and theatre artist. The author of six books and co-editor of three anthologies, he was the 2013 recipient of the Dayne Ogilvie Prize and a three-time Lambda Literary Award finalist. Formerly artistic producer of the frank theatre company and currently community engagement producer for CultureBrew.Art, he is the recipient of two Jessie Richardson Awards for his work as a theatre artist and producer. He is currently developing a new version of his play *Falling in Time* with director Peter Hinton-Davis. His memoir, *Double Melancholy: Art, Beauty, and the Making of a Brown Queer Man*, was published in 2019 by Arsenal Pulp Press. (Instagram: @ce_gatchalian; Twitter/X: @CEGatchalian; Facebook: @CEGatchalian; website: cegatchalian.com.)

It's Vancouver, Canada, 1994, the year of the deaths of two equally legendary but ostensibly unrelated individuals: North Korean dictator Kim Il-Sung and Nirvana band leader Kurt Cobain. Through all this, four distinctly different lives intertwine. Steve is an African American, bisexual Korean War vet whose open embrace of Western imperialistic values hides a haunted and tortured soul. Jamie is an aloof young Filipino Canadian writer struggling with self-hatred and feelings of emptiness. Chang Hyun is a young mixed-race Korean ESL student brimming with anti-Western sentiment and reeling from a traumatic experience in the military. In the middle of it all is Eun Ha, a Korean woman who lived through the Korean War and, against all odds, found the will to survive.

Steve is living in Metro Vancouver, drowning his troubles in a sports bar, while revealing hidden depths, including some family history and his love for Joe Louis and Billie Holiday.

Falling in Time was first produced by the frank theatre company (then called Screaming Weenie Productions) in Vancouver on November 4, 2011. It was performed by Manami Hara, Kevin Kraussler, Allan Morgan, Nelson Wong; directed by Sean Cummings; with set and lighting design by Itai Erdal; costume design by Christopher David Gauthier; sound design by Mike Rinaldi; and stage management by Jethelo Espaldon Cabilete.

✦✦✦

STEVE is in a bar, on a stool, drink in hand, inebriated.

People talking and laughing, glasses clinking, etc. Billie Holiday singing "On the Sunny Side of the Street" in the background.

STEVE: Watch it now. You are talking about a legend, a lady, *the* Lady . . . Never liked her voice? Well she never liked yours, either! . . . Seriously, the prettiest voice ain't usually the best. Pretty voices are a dime a dozen. But a voice like Billie's—it's the voice of humanity. Her voice ain't pretty coz humanity ain't pretty. You can either frill around the truth, or be brave and just *be* it. She didn't need four octaves; she didn't need no fancy notes. She said more with one note than other singers say in ten. She's what the Yorùbá call an orisha. A deified ancestor. Just started reading up on it. A bona fide orisha.

Lights snap out then up again. He has become more inebriated.

Joe Louis, the Brown Bomber. Saw him win his last title just a coupla years before Korea. Made the trip to New York from Birmingham just to watch Joe fight. Wasn't the fighter he used to be, no one thought he could win . . . but no matter. The man was beautiful. I *had* to go see him. A hero, *my* hero . . . he was *someone*, know what I mean? I was eight when I first heard of him. Schmeling and Louis, the fight of the century. For a moment, there was *something else* to pay attention to. Germany versus America. White versus Black. For a moment America was me, a brother, a Black man. That same year my father's drinking buddy was lynched in Mississippi. But a moment is all it took. Louis knocked the kraut down three times in two minutes. The Brown Bomber atop the world, and there was God, just for a moment. So yeah, I had to see him. So in nineteen hundred and forty eight I spent my life savings on a flight to New York to see him fight Jersey Joe Walcott. I was there, close to the ring, but not too close, know what I mean? Close enough to know he was real, but not *too* close to spoil anything. Fuck how he danced, how he danced in that ring. Got me through Korea, the memory of that fight. A memory like a diamond, something they couldn't break.

> *Lights snap out, one-count. Lights up. He is now even more inebriated, but speaks with fierce clarity.*

No, I'm not "visiting" from Seattle. I've lived in this damn city for twenty-two years. Dammit, if I had a nickel for every time someone asked me if I'm a tourist . . . So what if I had a crush on Joe fucking Louis. I am indeed a faggot, a sodomite, a fudge packer. I would indeed love to part your Surrey-boy white ass and shit-stab you senseless, right here, right now. Can't handle it? Bothered? Threatened? Outraged? Just remember I'm a *Black* faggot so my rage alone can break your neck. Just keep that in mind before you throw me out.

AGOKWE

WAAWAATE FOBISTER

MIKE: Here we go, Mike. The big game! You can kill this game. Kill those Beavers. We'll show them. Remember, Windigo can kill beaver any day because beavers are creatures of habit. They always play too hard at the beginning and wear themselves out. That's their weakness. I don't gotta do much at the beginning. Just let them wear themselves out and go in for the kill. That's why you're the hunter; just like Mom. The beaver is your prey tonight. Pfffft. That's the difference between you and Douglas Big Canoe. You're the hunter and he's a drunk. If Mom wasn't such a good trapper we would have starved. What use is a big canoe when it's sunk at the bottom of a bottle? Useless fucker—me and Mom are better off without you. We'll see who's the man around here. I'm the man. I'm the man. I'm the man. I'm the man. I am the fuckin' man.

He breaks and cries.

Fucking pussy.

TIME, AND THE WRITING AND REWRITING OF *FALLING IN TIME*; OR, PISSING WHITE PEOPLE OFF; OR, BORN AGAIN*

C.E. GATCHALIAN

In 2005, I started writing a play called *Falling in Time*. Seventeen years later, I'm still writing it.

This essay is about my seventeen-year journey with this play, replete with self-hate, erasure, an agonizing and necessary death, and a spiritual and political rebirth.

✦✦✦

I started writing *Falling in Time* in January 2005. I wrote it while I was playwright-in-residence at the Firehall Arts Centre in Vancouver. I had just received my first Canada Council grant, so I was brimming with the confidence of a "validated" artist.

The year prior, I had worked as an ESL conversation tutor in Vancouver, teaching mostly Japanese and Korean students. This experience formed the autobiographical springboard of *Falling in Time*, from which I created storylines set during the Korean War and 1990s Vancouver.

No one has ever accused me of not being single-minded, and in the early years of writing *Falling in Time*, I had but one life goal: getting this play produced.

---

* A slightly different version of this essay was presented at fu-GEN Theatre's GENesis 2022: Pocket Conference (Vancouver edition) on November 25, 2022.

If I were smarter and less capitalistically inclined, I wouldn't have been so dead set on being produced. I'd embrace and be satisfied with the process for its own sake, and regard production as a consequence rather than a primary.

That said, I'll concede that desiring to share and communicate one's stories to others isn't a capitalist impulse—it's part of the human impulse to connect.

So I concede that the impulse is genuine, though it's perverted by the machinery of capitalism to modify, cut, make more palatable, and in my case, whitewash.

To get produced in professional theatre means, more often than not, to whitewash.

✦✦✦

Falling in Time has four main characters: Chang Hyun, a Korean ESL student; Eun Ha, his grandmother; Steve, an ailing Korean War veteran; and Jamie, an ESL tutor. In its original iteration, the latter two characters are white, including the ESL tutor.

As I mentioned, my work as an ESL tutor formed the play's autobiographical springboard. The character of the ESL tutor is clearly my surrogate. And yet I wrote that character as a white person.

Why?

It simply didn't occur to me that this was at all problematic. That writing myself as a white person could be a sign of something being not quite right. I had imbibed wholesale the notion that race doesn't matter, that we live in a post-racial world.

But there was another, more practical reason. Eleven years ago, it would have been almost impossible to find a Filipino queer actor, even simply a Filipino actor of any sexual orientation, based in Vancouver, to play this role.

As I said, I had but one life goal at the time: to get this play produced. *More often than not, to produce is to whitewash.*

✦✦✦

So the play was produced. *Falling in Time* had its world premiere in Vancouver in November 2011.

By all conventional standards, it was a success. It played to 80 per cent houses across its two-week run. It generated buzz and some laudatory reviews. It was published the year after by Scirocco Drama. And it won and was shortlisted for some major awards.

But there was something missing.

While it was a beautiful production, it usually takes two or three iterations before a play truly hits its stride, both production-wise and writing-wise, and *Falling in Time* was no different. So I knew I wasn't done with it. And I was intent on getting it produced elsewhere, preferably in Toronto—where, as a Canadian playwright, I understandably wanted to make my mark.

There was still something missing. The reasons I just articulated don't address that missing thing. I wouldn't be able to pinpoint it until eight years later.

✦✦✦

In 2018, I connected with Peter Hinton-Davis, a very fine and accomplished director based in Ontario. I gave him the original version of *Falling in Time* to read, and he liked it. We started discussing a revised version of the play, with the end goal of a new production in mind.

The following year, I secured a creation residency with a theatre company, which allowed me a concentrated amount of time to rewrite the play. Together, Peter and I worked on the play via regular Zoom meetings during the pandemic, culminating in a weeklong in-person workshop in March.

The new version of the play is forty-five minutes shorter, and, structurally, immeasurably tighter and more intentional than the original. But for the purposes of this essay, what matters is how I have rethought the characters, so this is where I will turn my focus now.

There are two Korean characters in the play: Chang Hyun, the ESL student, and Eun Ha, his grandmother. In the original version I didn't bring in a Korean cultural consultant until we were in rehearsals for the production. This was a mistake on my part. I should have worked with a Korean cultural consultant right from the get-go. So for the new version of *Falling in Time*, I corrected this wrong. From the outset, before I started the actual rewriting of the play, I engaged Maki Yi, a Vancouver-based Korean Canadian theatre artist, who has not only written the Korean passages in the new version—approximately 30 per cent of the script is now in Hangul—but also dove into deep, nuanced conversations with me about gender and sexuality in a Korean cultural context.

The character of Steve, the Korean War veteran, was originally written as a white man. After a lot of introspection and some fear on my part, I decided to write Steve as African-American in the new version. Steve is, to put it crassly but not inaccurately, the play's ugly American. I thought it would be an interesting and nuanced choice to reimagine him as Black, as a marginalized person who has imbibed the doxas of American imperialistic racial capitalism and has, in effect, become its most vociferous champion. For this part of the project, I engaged Diane Roberts, formerly artistic director of Urban Ink in Vancouver and now a freelance director and dramaturge based in Montréal. Diane's dramaturgy was invaluable, gently but assertively pointing out the blind spots in my depiction of Steve, specifically how the world reacts and responds to him as a *Black* man.

The fourth main character in *Falling in Time* is Jamie, the ESL tutor, who is, for all intents and purposes, me. Jamie was always the blandest, least interesting character in the play's original version. Looking back, it was inevitable that this would be the case, and it's inextricably linked to why I didn't start reading Filipino intellectuals and activists until this year. I will circle back to this in a bit.

I had long conversations with Peter Hinton-Davis about this character, convos which culminated in Peter asking me the following question, which, considering how smart he is, I know was rhetorical:

"Is Jamie you?"

Iyan. Ay talaga.

You know how, quite often, the biggest epiphanies concern truths that are literally right under your nose? They're so obvious, you don't see it. Truth is paradox. Buddhist teachers and meditators talk about this all the time.

So, without forcing anything on me, Peter facilitated my rewriting the character of Jamie as a young queer Filipino man. Jamie is essentially me when I was twenty years old.

This triggered me to introspect about why I was so cavalier when I originally worked on this play about writing this character as white, and why it never even occurred to me that this was problematic.

I turned forty-eight this June. *I didn't start reading about pre-colonial Filipino culture until this year.*

And writing Jamie as me—fully me—was the catalyst that, after seventeen years, fully opened the play up to me, allowing me to really delve deep, no holds barred, into the issues the play explores, in a way I wasn't able to when I originally wrote it.

I'm not self-flagellating about this. I accept that the lion's share of this was not actually within my control. We are historical beings. As much as we have agency, we are also conduits for the prevailing philosophies of the times we happen to be in.

The world is whitewashed. It was particularly so when I was growing up—the words "decolonizing" and "microaggression" weren't on anybody's radar, except perhaps for a faction of the academic elite. The beauty and desirability standards I grew up with were white. The TV shows, movies, and plays I devoured were white. The books I read were all in English and written by mostly European and American authors. My crushes were always white and I aspired to snag a white boyfriend. My white classmates, friends, peers, and fellow artists would dismiss any and all claims I made about racist treatment as exaggeration, overreaction, ego, or simply being in a bad mood. Not only was I invisible, I was also over-sensitive and likely delusional.

With this in mind, is it any wonder that I had no interest in writing about myself?

✦✦✦

For most of my life, I've been blind to my own Filipino-ness.

A single-minded desire to succeed in a white world, and in a white-dominated art form, made me indifferent to anything that would not directly advance my position in it.

Racial capitalism did a number on me, as it has with so many BIPOC folx. It alienated me from my own ancestral power.

But not completely.

Even the deeply, thoroughly colonized playwright who started writing *Falling in Time* seventeen years ago took a weird, decidedly non-linear approach to time in the play. To this day he still can't wholly articulate the reasons behind this impulse, but the words of Filipino-American thinker Leny Mendoza Strobel come as close as any to elucidating them:

> *The Filipino notion of time is mythical, nonlinear, celebratory—the convergence of the past and the future into an eternal present, where everything occurs all at once, clues us in on why the Filipino index of happiness is high; why we find humor in the most dire situations, why we suffer long. This is also why our critics castigate us and try to whip us into more disciplined habits, only to be continually frustrated.*
>
> —Leny Mendoza Strobel,
> *Babaylan: Filipinos and the Call of the Indigenous*

✦✦✦

The world has changed in the last eleven years.

Falling in Time deals with toxic masculinity, a concept that wasn't even part of our collective vocabulary eleven years ago. The audience can now bring something to the play that they couldn't when the play was originally produced.

There is also greater openness in talking about race issues than there was eleven years ago. Growing numbers of people now recognize that white supremacy isn't just about people wearing white hoodies and carrying burning crosses—it includes all varieties of subtler aggressions as well, both sociopolitical and personal.

Slowly but surely, the Canadian stage is getting browner. Barring natural disaster or anything completely unforeseen, I can say with a fair amount of certainty that it will indeed be a Filipino queer actor playing Jamie in the next production of *Falling in Time.*

✦✦✦

Another thing that's changed: I care way less about pissing white people off.

I've had my share of battles over this new version of *Falling in Time*, which is not about racism, but *white supremacy*, and has not a single white character on stage.

Walang hiya. No shame.

The straight white company dramaturge I was working with on the play—who shall remain nameless—went AWOL on me after the workshop, jettisoning their responsibilities and ghosting me for two months before admitting, after I cornered them, that they just didn't get the "why" of the play and was therefore removing themselves from the project. When I called this person in, inviting them to meet with me privately to discuss our differences, they said no. So I summoned this response:

> You saying that you "don't fully grasp the 'why'" of my play is akin to saying that you don't fully grasp "why," as a queer human being of colour, I exist.
>
> There are many "white," "straight" plays that I don't understand the rationale for producing, because I am not reflected in them and they are not personally relevant to me. Yet white straight people continue to produce them anyways, and queer BIPOC folx who are hired on them are obligated to do the work they are paid for and have committed to doing. I regret that you missed the double standard there.

Another white person who read the play emailed me this response:

> My first read of the play just made me angry with its preachiness. White man bad. Asian man and Black man good. It struck me as remarkably unbalanced. And I hope the audience speaks Korean or are the songs and poems to be translated? Didn't find any nuance and apart from the sex scenes, I suppose the gay or bi (or whatever the politically correct term today is) I'm guessing they/we are a misunderstood minority too. I'm certain Peter Hinton can probably make it work for audiences who are predominantly us white colonizing imperialistic capitalistic villains . . . Sorry, Chris, I was expecting something totally different but not so one-sided . . . I think it was Samuel Goldwyn who said: "If you want to send a message, use Western Union!"😄😄

To be fair to this person, they have told me that they are keeping an "open mind" and that they genuinely want to understand and grasp what the play is getting at. I believe them.

Sigi na. Let's dive in and have the difficult conversations. I'm all for that. Enough with the polite tiptoeing that has far too often been the modus operandi in Anglo Canadian theatre.

It's worth noting that seventeen, or even ten, years ago, my response to these white people's critiques would have been to give them credence and, probably, acquiesce to them.

Today my response is, in the words of one of my favourite white dudes of all time, Kurt Cobain, *whatever.*

✦✦✦

I came out as queer in my early twenties, and truly thought that, by coming out, I had solved all my problems. After all, wasn't the gay world completely devoid of bigotry? Weren't hierarchies of any kind non grata in queerdom?

Perhaps that's why I found queer white supremacy so much more painful than the standard brand. The party I ended up at was not the one I thought I was invited to.

Truth is paradox. The world in which I came of age sexually was also the world whose white supremacy sharpened my race consciousness.

In the past, when pressed, I would identify as a queer artist first, an artist of colour second. While ultimately I am disinclined to hierarchize my identities, these days, when pressed, I identify as brown first, queer second—the result of being burned by white queer racism.

White supremacy is ubiquitous, its tendrils extending even to ostensibly welcoming spaces. That said, it has been in racially mixed queer spaces that I have felt most free to have the hard conversations. In general—with notable exceptions—I have found white queers to be far less fragile than white straights. The "drama queen" (or "drama monarch"!) label is something I'm learning to embrace; the truth is, in appropriate contexts, "bringing the drama" can help effect necessary change.

Ultimately, it is still in queer spaces where I feel most completely myself, and where I am most able to hold the tensions necessary to generate truth.

✦✦✦

Something happened the other day while I was thinking about and working on this presentation.

I experienced a death.

Triggered by memories of past personal and professional trauma, of toxic white authority figures dismissing, disregarding, undermining, and gaslighting me because I present as a soft-spoken, accommodating, and easygoing person, my body erupted in shivers. I had trouble functioning that whole day.

The anger was all consuming. *The body remembers.* Centuries of colonization, of my ancestors being told on both the conscious and subliminal levels that they weren't good enough, that their brown skin made them "naturally" inferior but that with the right education and religion they could become reasonable facsimiles of white folx.

I felt like punching the wall in. *The body never forgets.*

I realized that all the standards of excellence that I have upheld and worked towards my entire life have been inextricably attached to whiteness and physicalized in white bodies.

I also realized that my addiction to the secret fantasy of these white authority figures one day apologizing to me is yet another form of white-centring.

Tama na. Enough.

The only solution: to de-spotlight whiteness completely and commence with a whole new paradigm.

Jamie is Filipino. I am Filipino.

It's been a destabilizing period, full of agony and self-doubt, moving in the world without the usual crutches.

But here I am.

Born and raised on the unceded territories of the Musqueam, Squamish, and Tsleil-Waututh peoples (colonially known as Vancouver), now based primarily in Tkarón:to (Toronto), C.E. Gatchalian (he/him/his) is a Filipinx diasporic queer author and theatre artist. The author of six books and co-editor of three anthologies, he was the 2013 recipient of the Dayne Ogilvie Prize and a three-time Lambda Literary Award finalist. Formerly artistic producer of the frank theatre company and currently community engagement producer for CultureBrew.Art, he is the recipient of two Jessie Richardson Awards for his work as a theatre artist and producer. He is currently developing a new version of his play Falling in Time *with director Peter Hinton-Davis. His memoir,* Double Melancholy: Art, Beauty and the Making of a Brown Queer Man, *was published in 2019 by Arsenal Pulp Press. (Instagram: @ce_gatchalian; Twitter/X: @CEGatchalian; Facebook: @CEGatchalian; website: cegatchalian.com.)*

CHAPTER 4
ANAGNORISIS

NOCTURNE (AN INCOMPLETE AND INACCURATE ACCOUNT OF THE LOVE AFFAIR BETWEEN GEORGE SAND & FREDERIC CHOPIN)

TANYA MARQUARDT

Tanya Marquardt (they/them) is a writer and performer. Their work is intimate, including memoirs, TED talks/seances, private dances, "texting plays," MP3 meditations, epistolary performances written to dream lovers—a fierce mucking about with vulnerability to get at life as a former runaway, third-generation Magyar settler, and genderqueer. Tanya's book *Stray: Memoir of a Runaway* (Little A, 2018) was named a Best Queer & History Bio by *The Advocate* and was adapted into a punk musical with Tim Carlson and Theatre Conspiracy. Their plays include *Nocturne (an incomplete and inaccurate account of the love affair between George Sand & Frederic Chopin)*; *Transmission*; and *Some Must Watch While Some Must Sleep*, a play about being a sleep talker, which became the basis for a story on NPR's *Invisibila*. Their performances have been presented at the PuSh Festival, the Vancouver International Dance Festival, FOLDA, Dancing on the Edge, rEvolver, and SummerWorks, among others. Awards include a 2022 Pushcart Prize nomination, the 2007 Sydney J. Risk Emerging Playwright Award, a 2010 Vancouver Mayor's Arts Award, and a shortlist nomination for the CBC Literary Awards. They currently live and work in Salish Territories/Vancouver and Lenapehoking/Brooklyn.

A contemporary retelling of a classic queer romance, *Nocturne (an incomplete and inaccurate account of the love affair between George Sand & Frederic Chopin)* is the love story between Fred, an ailing musician and George, a genderfluid writer. Neighbours in a New York apartment, George steals into Fred's window one night to hear his music, and leaves with his heart. Later, when Fred is unable to satisfy George's sexual needs, she creates a role-playing game in the hopes of seducing him, becoming a servant that Fred is in charge of every night. But when the game starts turning sour, both Fred and George must risk seeing each other for who they really are.

In the following monologue, George tells Fred about a memory of trying to find the "right" washroom at a public pool.

Nocturne (an incomplete and inaccurate account of the love affair between George Sand & Frederic Chopin) was first produced at the Walking Fish Festival, Vancouver, in May 2003. It was performed by Heather Doerksen and Frano Marsic.

✦✦✦

GEORGE: I walked into the wrong washroom once. At the pool. I was seven, not that being seven was an excuse, but I was seven, and I was taking swimming lessons. I remember I had a black bathing suit, but that's beside the point. At the end of my lessons, I walked towards the bathroom. I looked up. One sign said "Women" with an arrow pointing THAT WAY. Another sign said "Men" with an arrow pointing THAT WAY. The arrows seemed very clear. But I was confused. It seemed strange to me that THAT WAY would lead me to the women's washroom—particularly because my body just felt wrong about the whole thing. But I couldn't articulate it then. So there I was looking up and feeling wrong and for some mystical reason I walked THAT WAY. The tiles were blue and misty, like being in a cloud. I walked down a short corridor, made a sharp right, walked down a longer corridor, a sharp left, and was met by the sharp, shrill girlish screams of twelve-year-old boys covering their penises. They looked as if someone had come to take their penises away. I just stared at them. I turned around calmly and walked back to the signs. "Which way is my way?" I thought to myself. I was so confused. I stood there for a long time just staring at the signs, and then in one direction, and then the other.

HYMN OF THE WEAVER BIRDS

JOHNNY WU

Johnny Wu (he/him) is a bilingual Taiwanese Canadian interdisciplinary artist. Graduating from Simon Fraser University with a double major in Theatre Performance and Criminology, his work seeks to investigate humanity through storytelling with social consciousness. Johnny believes storytelling, on stage or screen, allows us to witness diverse lived experiences from an empathetic mind, which catalyzes social change—understanding is the key and storytelling is the hand that turns the key. Johnny's theatre credits include *The Pink Line: Pain Held Tight* (2016), *these violent delights* (2017), *Portrait of My DNA* (2020), *Relearning Filial Piety* (2021), and *MH370* (2021). His screen credits include *Bunny Man* (2018), the CW Network's *Legends of Tomorrow* (2020) and *Kung Fu* (2021), and Liongate's *Joy Ride* (2023). Johnny is also the vice president of the board at PuSh International Performing Arts Festival as well as a sessional lecturer at Toronto Metropolitan University.

Six Asian queer men serendipitously find themselves in the same abandoned apartment in Taipei City. Broke, devious, and each with their own axe to grind, they all refuse to leave. Thus begins a soul-searching fantasia that takes them on a retrospective journey revisiting stories of their past and the traumas they refuse to face. Woven into their stories are memories of women in their lives—sisters, mothers, grandmothers—who've lost their way due to the shackles of traditional feminine conventions, ways of life the men so desperately rejected or sought to escape. With minds and spirits scarred, the men ruminate on femininity and what they end up uncovering is an inspired insight into the essence of the human heart.

The Writer is a hopeless romantic whose life's mission is to find "true love." He would fall into different relationships and document his experience in his novels under the guise of fiction. Yet the onset of a cruel illness seeks to topple his whole expedition. He retraces his steps, revisiting past lovers—one by one—hoping to unravel what went wrong in each relationship. And now, he is facing his first love. The tension comes to a climax as the Writer confronts his jealousy of this lover's ability of "just being themselves." They aren't desperate enough for love to fake their way through life as the Writer does. It's a moment of self-reflection masked by emotional projection.

✦ THE WRITER ✦

WRITER: Maybe you're right . . .
I am jealous
I'm jealous of you
I'm jealous of the birds
I'm jealous of the trees
I'm jealous of the fishes that just get to swim to wherever the fuck they want to go.
I'm jealous of everything and everyone that *isn't* me.
I'm jealous of *that.*
I'm jealous of people who just . . .
get to *be* . . .
I'm so fucking fed up and I'm so fucking jealous of people who just get to be themselves.
How wonderful . . .
How nice it must be . . .
How nice it must feel . . .
to love the skin you're in.
To be able to walk the earth every single day
and to be like, "Oh yeah, okay, this is me today."
I'm jealous of that.
Because I want that so fucking bad . . .
I . . . I . . . I want that *so much.*
I'm jealous of people who just know they are loved,
who don't have to question it
who don't have to check themselves in the mirror every single hour to make sure that they still look beautiful *enough* to be loved.
Or that their stomach is still flat enough.
Or that their face is still young enough.
Or whatever the fuck we *have* to be.
Just to be loved.
. . .

I am jealous
and I don't want to be.
And that . . .
that is what I'm most jealous about:
is not having *to be jealous.*
. . .
is to know that you are good enough
to know that you are loved enough
that you don't have to look at someone else and feel like you want their life.
That is what I'm jealous of:
It's people that get to live . . .
as anything else other than *this*,
other than me.
So, yeah.
I guess . . .
This is it.
This is me.
So maybe I am jealous
maybe I'm just a monster who is envious of everything in this fucking goddamn world
but *you* can't blame me for it.
You can't blame me for it.
You can't hate me for it.
You can't dislike me for it
You have to give me mercy for it.
Even if I am jealous.
You still have to love me.
Because you will never understand how much it hurts to be jealous.

HEARTLINES

SARAH WAISVISZ

Sarah Waisvisz (she/her) is a playwright, director, and multidisciplinary performer with training in dance and physical theatre (classical ballet, puppetry, acrobatics, stilts, and West African dance styles). Her solo script *Monstrous*, about the Afro Caribbean Jewish-diaspora experience and mixed-race identity, was published in *alt.theatre* and performed at b current's rock.paper.sistahz festival in Toronto and across Canada and the US. Her epic two-act, surrealist play *Heartlines*—about the life, love, and resistance work of Claude Cahun and Marcel Moore—had a sold-out run at Ottawa's Great Canadian Theatre Company (GCTC). In December 2023, *Heartlines* was published by Methuen Drama (Bloomsbury) in an anthology entitled *Global Jewish Plays: Five Works by Jewish Playwrights from Around the World*. She is currently working on *Double Helix*, an Afrofuturist, magical-realist play about the African diaspora, and she directed Donna-Michelle St. Bernard's *Witness Shift* for Obsidian Theatre and CBC Arts as part of the award-winning filmed anthology *21 Black Futures*. Sarah is an assistant professor at the DAN School of Drama and Music at Queen's University.

Queer Jewish lovers flee the fascism of WWII and find resistance buried deep in their respective artistic disciplines in *Heartlines*. Using play-within-a-play autobiographical storytelling, real-life artists and queer lovers Marcel Moore (born Suzanne Malherbe) and Claude Cahun (born Lucy Schwob) take the audience through the dizzying romance of their carefree early life together in Paris, and the fracturing and fragmenting of that life with the rise of Hitler and antisemitism during WWII. Identities of all kinds—gender, sexual, religious, national, creative—are explored, negotiated, suppressed, oppressed, and liberated as Claude and Suzanne invoke their surrealist art through dangerous acts of resistance to the Nazi regime.

Claude is based on the historic person Claude Cahun a.k.a. Lucy Schwob. In writing this character the playwright tried to give voice to Claude's artistic and personal exploration of gender. In their time and place, there is no language to adequately describe who they are in the world. In this monologue, Claude tries to describe who they are, even though they know that those who consider themselves to be "normal" will never understand. They try anyway.

Heartlines was first produced by Calalou and RAFT Theatre Projects as part of the TACTICS Mainstage Series at Ottawa's GCTC from March 24 to April 3, 2022. It was performed by Maryse Fernandes (Suzanne), Margo MacDonald (Claude), and Scottie Irving (Bandleader). The play was directed and dramaturged by Rebecca Benson; with lighting design by Tristan-Olivier Breiding; stage management by Rebecca Eamon Campbell; video mapping by Andrew Galligan; production management by Christine Hecker; costume design by Vanessa Imeson; sound design and music by Scottie Irving; visual art collaboration by Kim Kielhofner; intimacy coaching by Megan Piercey Monafu; set and prop design by Andrea Steinwand; and assistant stage management by Arielle Voght and Yutong Ngui Wei.

✦ OUTSIDER ✦

CLAUDE: If you've always felt *normal* then you can't begin to understand what it feels like to know you are Other. Different. Eventually in Paris I met other women and men who never felt like they belonged: they were Jews, or Blacks, *métisses*, or queers; often they were artists. They kept travelling, kept running, kept performing, kept writing—always on the fringes no matter where they landed. But there will always be someone who refuses to hide, who refuses to wear a skirt or be married off. For me, it's like my body never matched me. As a girl I tried to match me to my body, but it felt like the inside of my head was on fire every time I acted like a good little girl. So to stop the feeling of the fire in my head I stopped trying to match me to my body: I wore a girl's school uniform but I wore *tzizit* under my blouse, put a *kippah* on my head . . . I wanted to be like the Jewish boys at religious school, learn what they were learning . . . But it got me in trouble; first it was just teasing from those boys, and then one day some *goyish* kids tied me to a tree and pelted me with rocks. After that my father sent me to boarding school in England. But I got into a different kind of trouble there, and I was dragged home to go to the local *lycée*. That's when I met Suzanne. The ultimate betrayal was my own body. How would I stop that bleeding every month? I couldn't believe how wasteful it was: all that blood and pain and I knew even then that I never wanted to be a mother, never wanted a man near me. But my breasts, my hips, my belly, my thighs . . . so soft and rounded—as if to spite me. I wondered how thin I would have to get until my woman's body disappeared. I knew I could make my breasts disappear under tight bandages or cloth, but how could I get rid of them forever? Don't get me wrong: I didn't want to be a man. I just didn't want to be a woman. Could I be neither? I didn't want a prick, I just didn't want to live in this soft body—I never did— Was there another option? A third option? The space and possibility of a third sex excited me. An in-between space between man and woman. A third sex. Neuter. Not feminine or masculine. Not *femme* or *homme* but *neutre*. That's what I knew I was. And I was certain there were others like me. But in Nantes? I felt utterly alone. Even after I met Suzanne.

FREDA AND JEM'S BEST OF THE WEEK

LO FINE

In alphabetical order, Lo Fine (all pronouns welcome) is an accountant, artist, bubby, butch being, daddio, friend, Jew, mom, non-bio parent, optimist, partner, playwright, queer, songwriter, treasurer, white settler, worrier, young senior. Wishing to give thanks to Bilal and Evan for all the hard work in putting this resource together.

Freda and Jem's Best of the Week is a story of a lesbian divorcée with kids. Are the kids all right? Maybe or maybe not. Freda and Jem have grown apart and Jem finds herself feeling like a relic. Her butch identity is all she knows and she hangs onto it as Freda moves forward. They are a family and will continue to be one, especially for the kids, but in the end Jem stands alone.

Jem is an old-school butch who came of age in the bar scene when roles for butches and fems were much more defined. Once she met Freda and they decided to have kids, Jem can't believe her good fortune to be able to be a parent. It is a role she embraces with all her heart. However, in the end, Freda and Jem split apart and Jem is left to make sense of the world and her place in it.

Freda and Jem's Best of the Week was first produced by Buddies in Bad Times Theatre, Toronto, on September 14, 2019. It was performed by Kathryn Haggis, Diane Flacks, Sadie Epstein-Fine, and Stephen Joffe; directed by Judith Thompson; with stage management by Sharon DiGenova; and music by Lorraine Segato.

✦ JEM ✦

JEM: I am a butch dyke. Think about it like this—I'm not a girl, I'm a boy. I'm not a man, I'm a woman. Us butches—we recognize each other on the street—but we don't say anything—that would be like breaking the butch code—but there's something—it's in the eyes—a look that passes between us—and we wonder in that moment about each other—what happened to you?—did you find someone to love you?—did you let her touch you deep down inside?—did you manage to hang on to her?—or did she leave you in the dust with her name on your tongue?

It wasn't easy being a little baby butch in the suburbs. The kids started saying I had tendencies. I hated that. Tendencies. They used the other word too in front of that. Lesbian. Lesbian. Tendencies. Those two words—I mean each of them on their own is bad enough—but together. Lesbian. Sounds like martian. Or alien. Or some creature—when I was sixteen I got a car and drove downtown. There was this bar—"The Virginia"—dark, smoky, full of women—the bathroom had these kind of saloon swinging doors—like what is that with that lesbian western motif—anyways I went inside and there was this old, grey-haired, grinning butch—grinning away at me—like she was seeing herself in me all over again—so what if I was too young to drink—she bought me beers that I drank with a straw—that big old grinning butch—we never even talked—just sat there—and I let her put her hand on my knee—at first it was okay, I told myself I could just let her do that—what was the harm—but after a while, her hand on my knee weighed a hundred pounds and her breath smelled rotten every time she let out a laugh—her little whispy moustache needed a trim badly and I thought—is this going to be my life—this hole in the wall that reeked of yesterday's bleach and an old crate of pickled eggs—the vinegar sticking in my throat all through my drive home—speeding down the Décarie Expressway with the windows wide open and the night air rushing at my ears—I'm in it too deep I thought—I'll never get out—I'd get home from that bar, close my bedroom door and take way too many aspirins—shut my eyes and wait for the dreams to come.

I never counted on kids. I didn't think that was ever going to be something that I would get to do. I knew I'd never get pregnant, but I didn't think I was going to ever even KNOW anyone pregnant, let alone be lovers with them—No sir, you came out into the bar scene in Montréal and you drank your beer and you had your job and you had a girlfriend if you were lucky—and the bar scene—it was hard core—the drinks cost twice as much and the liquor was only half as strong. The doors were locked with chains and you had to let the guard dogs sniff you to get in. The lights were red mostly, but if they ever turned white that meant the cops were raiding the place and you had to hightail it out of there as fast as you could. We never talked about kids back then—kids would ruin everything—kids would be like, what's the point of being a dyke if you're just going to do that—no we were living outside of the mould—we were revolutionaries—where were kids going to fit in all of that?—no you gave up all that notion and there was a point where you thought about it and it was kind of a relief, you know—no little noses to worry about—no teeth to put braces on—nobody to mess up your date night—nobody extra to fall in love with who could make you feel like you would have to die if you ever lost them—

TWICE

ISABELLE SANATDAR STEVENS

Isabelle (Fereshteh) Sanatdar Stevens (she/her) is a first-generation Iranian American who grew up in a family of immigrants and refugees from different countries and cultures. She is also a lesbian. These two aspects of her identity often manifest in her work, where she explores how different languages, cultures, and identities can intersect, overlap, and diverge. Perhaps a bit too curious, Isabelle writes as a way of finding and creating answers to questions she can't shake. Folklore and fantasy inspire her work, as the lines between reality and illusion are often blurred. A passionate theatre-maker, Isabelle loves performing improv, acting, writing, and working behind the scenes to make a show come to life. She is currently based out of Boston, Massachusetts, where she is a Playwriting M.F.A. candidate at Boston University.

Leyla, teens to early thirties, female-identifying, Middle Eastern, a lesbian. Leyla is thrown for a loop when her partner mentions her deceased father and what he would think of the person his daughter has become. (A version of herself that he will never have the chance to know.)

✦✦✦

LEYLA: Why?! Why would you say that? You had to know it would—"Your dad would be proud of you"—just throwing around phrases like the words are nothing! Empty words . . . weightless! You know what's not weightless? This anvil on my chest, hearing you say . . . You know *nothing* about my father! Nothing other than what I've told you. And how could you—you never even met him—how could you know that he'd be proud of me? Who gave you the right to speak for him like that? I'm sorry. I don't mean to—It's just . . . I'll never know, you know? I'll never . . . If he would be proud of me. It's a big if . . . HA! I was just a kid when he . . . and Iranians aren't really stereotyped as being "cool" when their daughters are into . . . Well, not men . . . I guess hearing you say that, I just . . . No one's ever said that before, or like, no one that I care about—no one who knows me. At least, not as well as you. I'd just shrug it off. Like, an auntie says it in passing, I smile. Nod. It's whatever—I know that they don't—that they're just saying what they feel in the moment . . . Or, or there's a stranger who . . . One time, an old lady—she stopped me in the street. I didn't know her, but I guess she knew my dad. She told me I had his face. She told me he would be proud of me. Proud of the "lovely young lady" I had become. It was inconsequential. Meaningless. I didn't care what she said—and I sure as hell knew she didn't know my father well enough to know what he would be thinking . . . But *you*! You know me! Better than anyone, even *him* at this point—and it's scary because for the first time, the words felt like they could be *real*. And I had to stop and . . . I had to stop and ask myself if I thought your words were true. If he really would be . . . proud . . . of me. Because I know he loved me then, but how could I know if he would love me now? How could I know if bringing my girlfriend home would be the line where unconditional love would become . . . hate. You've never lied to me before—maybe if you had it wouldn't have hit so hard—but you haven't. And . . . I guess I don't know if it's true. I'll never know. And not knowing almost feels harder than knowing. I mean, you always want to think you know that someone would have loved you . . . unconditionally.

But you can't, unless they tell you. And he hasn't told me . . . Well, because he can't. And it's hard because I love you. I love you and I love him and I'll never know if he were alive, if he'd still love me after finding out that I love you. And I want to keep loving you—I don't want to lose you. But I never wanted to lose him. And I never thought I could lose him again after he died, but hearing you say that I just . . . I just don't know . . . It almost feels like I've lost him twice.

ALMOND EYES

LYNNÉA CHAN

Lynnéa Chan (she/her) is a queer, Chinese Canadian theatre artist, vocalist, and graduate of the University of Victoria. Through writing, directing, and performance, Lynnéa hopes to create stories that are provocative, loving, and dedicated to casual diversity. Her creative interests include collaborative creation, experimental prose, grounded themes explored whimsically, and the legitimacy of genre fiction—specifically, fantasy, horror, and sci-fi. Theatrical credits include *The Children's Hour* (Phoenix Theatre), *Bad Dog* (Blue Jaye Productions), *It'll Come To Me* (Theatre SKAM), *Home Delivery Pop-Up Theatre* (Theatre SKAM), and *Ouroboros* (Hollow Hound Arts Collective). Lynnéa spends her spare time baking, bookbinding, making music, doing needlecraft, and rotating her ever-changing wheel of hobbies.

Almond Eyes is a ten-minute monologue about Wendy, a second-generation Chinese Canadian woman. Wendy has a strained relationship with her mother, her culture, and her womanhood. The play opens with Wendy taking a pregnancy test after an emotionally charged, irresponsible hookup. As she waits for the results, she reflects on her upbringing: she was raised by a strict single mother obsessed with avoiding racial stereotypes, which left her with a nebulous sense of self. Wendy recounts how easily she falls in love with various people who offer her insight into who she is, or who she could be. In the last moments of the play, Wendy discovers that she is in fact pregnant, and is woefully unprepared.

Wendy is a second-generation Chinese Canadian woman in her mid-twenties. She's got some shit to figure out. Wendy was raised by a single mother, with whom she has a fraught relationship. When she finds herself accidentally pregnant, Wendy must reflect on her upbringing and come to terms with her culture and womanhood.

Almond Eyes received a live-streamed staged reading as part of the Telling It Bent 2021 virtual showcase produced by the frank theatre company in Vancouver on May 21, 2021. It was performed by Katrina Teitz, directed by Patricia Trinh, with writing mentorship from Tawahum Bige.

✦✦✦

WENDY is watching the past, in a memory.

WENDY: At ten years old, I wait for my mom to pick me up from the community centre; I watch the hands on the clock go around and around. She's always late—it's two hours from here to home. There's a different community centre closer to home, but that one has a Chinese school attached. I know, because I see the shiny gold characters in the window. I saw a paper dragon once.

My mom says I'm lucky she's not sending me to Chinese school, but I don't think she's right. I dream about leaning over books with pencil stubs, tracing out the characters of a magic language, and the teacher who would read me Chinese tales out of books with the translation on one page and Chinese characters on the other. There'd be a real Chinese lady, like on TV, with the red dresses that go up to here—

WENDY indicates a cheongsam.

Not like my mom. My mom works at a jewellery store in the mall, and wears grey skirts and blazers. She does not look like the real Chinese Ladies on TV.

Before I spent most of my time here, I used to lie belly-down on the carpet and watch movies on TV. The family goes to a restaurant where a beautiful Chinese Lady serves tea. I tie my hair into a ponytail and stick chopsticks through the elastic band. My mom comes home and sees what I'm watching. She yells at me to shut it off:

"You're not allowed to watch this anymore, do you understand?"

I tell her I do, even though I don't, and I take the chopsticks out of my hair. I wish I could find out how the movie ends. The next week, she tells me our routine is going to change:

"McKayla's mom is going to pick you up after school, and take you two to the community centre downtown."

I tell her I don't want to go to the community centre downtown. I tell her I don't like McKayla. I ask my mom if I can go somewhere else. I could walk a block down by myself, to the centre there. I think if I got to meet a real Chinese Lady at Chinese school she would teach me so many things . . . the secrets behind the brush strokes I see in the window. Like a code.

Shift. WENDY *is nineteen, in a different memory.* WENDY *marvels—*

She speaks flawless Cantonese.

I am ashamed when I meet her and cannot tell the difference between Mandarin and Cantonese, cannot tell that the code she can speak in is my family's.

When I am nineteen, I work at a deli in a grocery store. I take the longest shifts I can, to get out of the apartment and away from my mother. I roll sushi, which everyone in the break room finds terribly appropriate. No one ever asks if I'm actually Japanese. There's another girl there, she works across the way in the bakery. She has beautiful blonde hair, and I never get close enough to see her eyes, but I imagine they are a sort of hazel-green colour.

She tells me she studied abroad in Hong Kong, and I drink up every detail of her studies there:

"Oh, shit, I've told you this story before, haven't I?"

"Tell me again, it's cool."

I wish I could be her; I wish I could live inside her body. She is me but inside out: a white girl inside a Chinese body. All of China behind her hazel eyes. I fall in love with her. I am a fetishist of my own culture.

UNEXPECTEDLY TRANS

HANLON UAFÁS-ÁLAINN

Hanlon Uafás-Álainn (he/they) is a transgender dad who writes, directs, produces, and performs for stage and screen. In 2012, Hanlon began writing monologues inspired by his personal exploration of gender—in mid-life, with small kids; this led to writing the play *Unexpectedly Trans* (with co-writer Mihály Szabados). *Unexpectedly Trans* inspired three films by Hanlon: *Holding Hands with the Awkward* (2018, co-written by Mihály Szabados), *Hamlet Moment* (2019), and *re:gen(d)eration* (2023), which won best feature at the East London LGBTQ+ Film Festival in London, England. Hanlon also wrote *Bubble Trans Pride*, with co-writer Syrus Marcus Ware (Halifax Fringe Festival, 2018; Rhubarb Festival, 2019). Currently, he has several works in various stages of development: *Inherited Beliefs* (feminist work set in rural NS, supported by the OAC, workshopped by Nightwood Theatre 2021), *Liminal idEntities* (a surreal dramedy), and *Call Me Papa* (supported by Roseneath Theatre, the Toronto Arts Council, the Ontario Arts Council, Lush Cosmetics, and individual donors). An adaptation of *Unexpectedly Trans*, *Call Me Papa* is a TYA play with music for young audiences that follows two siblings processing a parent's gender transition.

A forty-year-old birthparent of two begins to transition from a hetero-seeming woman to Dan, a queer, trans father. Dan must come out to his husband, children (aged five and seven), family, and community. Both big and small hearts are challenged by the real-life daily awkwardness of riding the TTC, shopping at the Eaton Centre, and going to the pool with kids—while trans. Dan, in the middle of his social and medical transition, is suffering from depression, dysphoria, and fears of being rejected, plus the day-to-day grind of continuously getting misgendered and belittled. He longs for acceptance, understanding, and peace of mind, but that all feels like it's a long way off. Dan also worries about the impact his transition is having on his young children; while seven-year-old Blair is super supportive, five-year-old Iris resists calling Dan "Papa." Even Dan's partner Drew struggles to understand his inner and outer battles. Dan is divided between hope and defeat as he entertains the idea of ending his life to escape the pain of existing while trans. So, Dan turns to his mirror-self with this dilemma. Little by little, Iris perceives that Dan is living his truth and by the end of the play she acknowledges, "Momma's gone . . . but I got the best Papa in the whole world."

Unexpectedly Trans was first produced by Hanlon's Point Productions, Iza's Productions, and 8 Monkeys Productions as part of Out Late (a double bill with *No Gold Star* by Alison Lynne Ward) at the Halifax Fringe Festival on August 21, 2017. It was written, directed, and performed by Hanlon Uafás-Álainn and Mihály Szabados; with set design by Jean Hanlon; music and lyrics for "Real Me" written by Hanlon Uafás-Álainn; musical accompaniment for "Real Me" arranged, performed, and recorded by Lisa St. Clair; and costume design for Angel Puss/Dan by Michael Legouffe.

✦ HAMLET MOMENT ✦

DAN is addressing his reflection in the empty mirror frame through which the audience peers.

DAN: We still have THOSE days, eh? You and I? When the task of doing what needs doing requires enormous effort. When those needling moments are so deflating. When I'm heart-weary, every unkind word is excruciating. We used to fantasize, didn't we? About going to the roof of a building and surrendering to gravity. The idea of escape from a world that feels hateful is a relief—for a moment—imagining the fall from those heights, sinking into the ground, like Neo in *The Matrix*.

The pain of every bone breaking at once.
The silence, the *freedom*!
The heartbreak.
No! That comes later.
Knowing that Drew, Blair, Iris would need us and we wouldn't be there . . . perhaps watching them suffer from the other side of the mirror—unable to hold them.
This is our Hamlet moment, yours and mine.
We both know we won't jump. It's just a fantasy—of escaping from the ugliness and pain.

But if we exert great effort of focus,
the comments and the glares, the threatening posturing,
are always overpowered by the unconditionality of the love we are given.
No matter what *gender* this body performs—I still get around in it, and there is always more love than hate to be had.

It's still tempting to run away!

Go to the forest. Wear a plaid shirt and chop wood.

LOST IN THE WOODS

AMANDA MERPAW

Amanda Merpaw (she/her) is a queer and disabled writer, editor, and educator. She is the author of *Most of All the Wanting* (Palimpsest Press) and *Put the Ghosts Down Between Us* (Anstruther Press). Her writing has appeared in a variety of literary magazines, including *carte blanche*, CV2, *Grain*, *long con*, *Plenitude*, *Prairie Fire*, and *Room*, and has been shortlisted for *Arc Poetry Magazine*'s Poem of the Year contest. As an artist-educator, Amanda has devised and produced performances for County Stage Company and the Kick & Push Festival. She is currently a contributing editor at *Arc Poetry Magazine* and a member of the editorial board at Anstruther Press.

Rae is feeling more existentially confused than usual. A divorced pansexual in her mid-thirties, she's developed a curious habit: characterizing her lovers (exes included) as trees. Or flowers. Herbs. Sometimes even fungi. She keeps track of all these characterizations in a notebook, with personalized drawings to boot. When the girl she's newly dating stumbles upon this notebook, Rae is furious. Not just because the girl read through it in close detail, but because she wants to know: what kind of tree would Rae be? And Rae hadn't considered that. So, after much inner turmoil, Rae records a submission to a relationship advice podcast to see if it might be able to help. Note: *Lost in the Woods* is a stand-alone monologue.

Rae (she/her): Thirty-something feminine pansexual. More comfortable in her head than in her body. A persistent self-talker. She frequently frames statements as questions to avoid being overly assertive—a kind of up-speak. Rae doesn't call her mother enough, but when she does, she usually cries. While Rae is written as a woman—she describes herself as such in the opening lines, and the stage directions use she/her pronouns—her gender can be shifted and played flexibly, differently, at the actor's discretion.

✦✦✦

RAE's place—she lives alone. Music plays from her phone. RAE, wearing a robe, dances around the room. She's nervous. She moves to the mirror, stares closely at her reflection. She stops the music. She closes her eyes for a moment and breathes deeply, intentionally, like she learned how to be calm from a meditation app. She opens the voice recorder on her phone and starts recording.

RAE: Hey! Hi! Um, long-time listener, first-time caller here. I just, I love your show, and I have a question, or a problem. I don't know, I'm not sure what it is.

Beat.

Ew. No. Absolutely not. Right. Okay. Take two.

RAE stops the first recording and starts another. She places her phone on a nearby surface. She slowly applies a full face of makeup in the mirror while recording a submission for a relationship advice podcast. She pauses the makeup application often to check how her face looks from a variety of angles.

Hi there! I'm a pansexual woman in my thirties calling from Toronto, Canada. I have a question for you about a conversation I had a few days ago with this woman I'm dating. It's pretty new, we started seeing each other a month ago. Maybe two? And she's . . . she's nice? She's good, a good person, I mean, and good to me, like, she plans these really fun, adventurous dates, not too adventurous, not dangerous or anything, just perfectly fun dates. We laugh a lot, which is sort of new for me? I always date these really serious people, these absolutely melancholy people, and she isn't that, which is so . . . refreshing. Yeah, refreshing.

So, she was over the other day and she had to pee. She was gone a long time so I went to check on her, right, I wanted to make sure she wasn't, like, crying for some reason? Or she hadn't . . . left? I don't know. I found her at my desk. You have to walk by it to get to the bathroom. She was looking at a notebook. At my notebook. It was open, I guess, I must've left it open, which is unlike me, but she said that it was sitting there like that. She was curious because of the drawings, so she looked. And then she kept looking.

It's a list, I guess? When it happened, when she read it, she seemed charmed at first, it didn't seem so bad, but then how it ended . . . People keep lists, right? In private places? She wasn't supposed to see. It's this list I keep of, uh, people I date? Lovers? Exes? Sometimes even the short-lived ones make the list, the one-dates, one-fucks, if I can think of what to call them, how to draw them. Not them, exactly, but them as a tree. Yes, like a tree tree. Like the ones in the forest. Or out in the yard. I mean, not my yard, I don't even have a yard, I live in a condo, but you know. Likes the ones on the street.

So yeah, I keep a list of which tree each of these people would be. It has their name, the person's name, then the tree I think they are, like, they're a water oak or an ash-leaf maple or a jack pine. It's actually pretty involved, you know? Considered, I mean. Are they deciduous or coniferous? What's their habitat, their ecosystem? What animals are drawn to them? How do they smell? Sometimes I can't think of a tree, it's pretty rare, but sometimes I can't, or maybe the person just . . . isn't a tree? They escape tree classification. So I list them as a flower instead, maybe an herb, sometimes a fungus. Everyone has a parallel. It's a way to remember or to make sense of or to hold on or to let go. It's like . . . therapy?

This girl, the one I'm dating, she's on the list. She's a beech tree from what I can tell so far, although I haven't figured out exactly what species yet. Beech feels right. It's the rustling of the leaves, the way they look in the light, dancing, almost leaping off their branches. They seem happy. She wasn't upset about being beech, about being a tree. And she shouldn't be, it's actually a really good one to be. More like . . . curious, I guess? She started asking all these questions, she had so many questions, she wanted to know about it all, about everyone, about my drawings, the trees. And I was furious. Mostly in that quiet way where you try not to show the other person, this new person, just how angry, how hurt, you have the capacity to be. She must've been standing there for so long, reading the list, turning the pages, without stopping herself, without thinking hard enough that it was private, that she was invading my space, invading me. Still, she kept going. And it's just not her business to know that the last girl I dated was an eastern redbud who needed space, always more space, or that after an extensive reflection process I realized my ex-husband was a bunch of rosemary.

Then she had the nerve to ask me what kind of tree I thought I was. To ask me. *(Long pause.)* I think she was flirting, I think she thought she was flirting with me. She asked almost . . . playfully. Like she was being whimsical or something? I lost it. I said, that's enough, I'm not going to talk to you about this, I'm not going to explain this to you, you've gone through my things, my private things, my mind, the deep parts of it that are not for you, not yet, and you haven't even apologized. You haven't even said sorry. Like, excuse me, but no, you don't get to know what kind of tree I am without at least an apology and some time for me to figure out how I even feel about the fact that this happened. Imagine! The audacity. She said she didn't realize it was a big deal. She thought it was cute, the trees, the drawings, she thought they were actually quite good. Her words, *quite good*, as though this was the time for an art review. She said she was sorry, she said the notebook was open on the desk when she walked by, she shouldn't have looked, she really was sorry. I said, I think you should leave now. And she did. She left.

> *RAE takes a moment to steady herself—a silent pep talk of a moment—before continuing.*

The thing is . . . I don't know what kind of tree I am. It's been a few days now and she's messaged to apologize, she's tried to call, she asks if she can see me again. I haven't responded because I don't actually know. I don't know the answer. How is that possible? I'm not even that mad anymore about the notebook. But how do I tell her that I haven't once thought about myself as a tree? Or as a flower, an herb, some fungus, whatever. I've spent years adding all these people, these ghosts, to this forest, and I don't know where I fit. How I'm planted. I don't want to ignore her but I don't think I can message her back until I know. How do I figure it out? I want to see her again. I like her. I think she's a good one. Beech trees really are one of my favourites.

> RAE *stops applying makeup. She picks up her phone. She speaks directly into it.*

So if you could help me out, that would be great. What should I do? How do I untangle this? What am I supposed to do? I'm hoping you can tell me, that you'll know.

> RAE *stares at the phone. She stops recording. She closes her eyes and breathes deeply, trying not to cry. She realizes she forgot one last step—maybe mascara or lipstick, some finishing touch—and she does it to complete the look, the moment. She walks away from the mirror to look for something to wear.*

THE GAY HERITAGE PROJECT

ANDREW KUSHNIR

Andrew Kushnir (he/him) is an actor, playwright, and director, as well as artistic director of the socially engaged theatre company Project: Humanity. His earliest forays as a performer/creator took place at Buddies in Bad Times Theatre via an alter ego named Captain Princess. Andrew's published plays include *The Middle Place* (Toronto Theatre Critics' Award); *Small Axe, Freedom Singer* (co-created with Khari Wendell McClelland); *The Gay Heritage Project* (co-created with Paul Dunn and Damien Atkins); and *Towards Youth: A Play on Radical Hope*. His play *The Division* was produced as part of the National Queer Theatre's 2023 Criminal Queerness Festival at Lincoln Center (NY). Andrew has long specialized in verbatim theatre and in 2021 brought his approach to an investigative theatre-history podcast he developed and hosted for the Arts Club entitled *This Is Something Else*. He is a Loran Scholar and graduate of the University of Alberta. In April 2022, he founded the We Support LGBTQ Ukraine Fund to help meet the needs of queer Ukrainians internally displaced or trapped by war. Visit kushnirandrew.com for more information.

Three queer creator/performers set out to answer one question: is there such a thing as a gay heritage? In their search, they uncover histories in the archival silences of the past and undertake a theatrical deep dive into contemporary queer culture. *The Gay Heritage Project* pays homage to those who've come before, to the nature of perspective and representation (across time and identity), and to the possibilities of community across differences. Created through a vocal masque technique, individual scenes—and each scene's myriad characters—are to be embodied by a solo performer in a highly physical, comedic and rapid-fire aesthetic. In this regard, the play is a three-headed, one-person show and a kind of queering of the standard theatrical monologue.

In this "solo scene," the vocal masque technique has one actor embodying five characters through zippy physical, vocal, and attitudinal shifts. The character of Gay Identity is doing his best straight drag, irony-free; Gay Desire is dripping with sarcasm, a stomach full of fire; Drag is flirty but firm; Camp is biting and mischievous; Joan Crawford is simply iconic. This scene is located in the third act (of five) in *The Gay Heritage Project*, entitled "Fight." This act grapples with the aftermath of the Toronto Police's "Operation Soap" steam bath raids, the "Fruit Machine" used to eliminate gay men from civil service in Canada, the wild and defiant use of Polari (a queer subculture language), and the ongoing violence 2SLGBTQ+ folks endure around the world.

The Gay Heritage Project was first produced by Buddies in Bad Times Theatre in Toronto on November 17, 2013. It was remounted and toured nationally in 2016. The play was written and performed by Damien Atkins, Paul Dunn, and Andrew Kushnir (albeit this scene was created by Andrew Kushnir), and directed by Ashlie Corcoran; with set and lighting design by Kimberly Purtell; sound design by Thomas Ryder Payne; projection design by Cameron Davis; and dramaturgy by J. Paul Halferty.

✦ THE GAY ALLEY ✦

City noises. GAY IDENTITY *moves through a dark alley, lost. He is on his cellphone.*

GAY IDENTITY: Yeah, I'll be right there. I took a bit of a wrong turn but . . . I think I've found a shortcut. Okay. See you soon.

As he hangs up, GAY IDENTITY *runs into someone lurking in the shadows.*

Oh.

GAY DESIRE: Hello.

GAY IDENTITY: Hi. I'm sorry. I'm trying to get downtown. Will *this* dark alley take me there?

GAY DESIRE: This one? Oh *sure*. You look dapper.

GAY IDENTITY: Oh. Thank you. I'm headed to a gala.

GAY DESIRE: A *gala*? Well, doesn't that sound nice. Say, you're Gay Identity, aren't you?

GAY IDENTITY: Uh, yeah. How did you know that?

GAY DESIRE: Well you're very recognizable. I don't suppose you remember *me*?

GAY DESIRE *finally steps into the light.*

GAY IDENTITY: Oh. You're . . . um—

GAY DESIRE: Desire. Gay Desire. It's been a minute. And surely you remember my sisters. This is Drag—

DRAG: *(stepping forward)* Hey, handsome.

GAY DESIRE: This is Camp—

CAMP: Well, if it isn't.

GAY DESIRE: And, of course, my third sister needs no introduction.

JOAN CRAWFORD waits.

GAY IDENTITY: Um— You're . . .

JOAN CRAWFORD: I'm Joan Crawford, goddammit.

GAY IDENTITY: Okay, look, I don't want any trouble—

GAY DESIRE: Awwww, come on, we're not here to pick a fight. We now fully understand why you threw us into the streets all those years ago. If the big gay assimilation project was going to have any chance, you had to clean house. And congratulations, by the way. Mission accomplished. Marriage equality and QSAs and gay characters on *every streaming service there is.*

GAY IDENTITY: You don't actually seem happy for me, Gay Desire.

GAY DESIRE: Apologies, Gay Identity. I'm a bit complicated. And I'm not very good at staying within one emotional state. Another reason not to keep me around.

GAY IDENTITY: Look. I didn't get rid of you guys. Not exactly. You're still a big part of who I am.

GAY DESIRE: Reallllly? It's hard to tell how, through all that straight drag you're doing.

GAY IDENTITY: I'm not doing drag.

DRAG: Oh, honey, we're all doing drag.

GAY IDENTITY: That's a really old-fashioned way of thinking.

CAMP: No, actually, it's a really *inclusive* way of thinking. The concept might *exceed* you, Gay Identity, but it *includes* you. Isn't that nice?

JOAN CRAWFORD: *(scandalized, à la Mildred Pierce)* I think I'm really seeing you for the first time in my life, and you're cheap and horrible.

GAY IDENTITY: All right, listen! The choices I've made have given us real political power. I managed to depathologize us, to get us rights like everyone else, and not just create tolerance, but acceptance.

GAY DESIRE: But, honey, did you look at the price tag? I mean, you essentially bankrupted the word gay to pay for it. You've reduced gay to something . . .

JOAN CRAWFORD: Flavourless, inoffensive, sexless.

DRAG: Middle-class, white.

CAMP: Why, you've reduced the word gay to a little adjective as opposed to a big, scary, messy, fisting verb.

GAY IDENTITY: That's what it took to make things change, and I'm proud of what we've accomplished.

GAY DESIRE: Yes, *proud*. You're certainly that. Why, you are *pride* incarnate. While we—we, on the other hand—we are effeminate; we are degenerate; we are diva-worship; we are youth-worship; we are narcissism; we are closets and park bushes and public restrooms; we are shadows and shame; we are loneliness; we are hopelessness; we are otherness; we are sentimentality, melodrama, glamour, self-proclaimed aristocracy; and we are obsessed, utterly *obsessed with our mothers*. We are all that feeling *and more*!

GAY IDENTITY: Well I'm not a mood—I'm a movement! And I did what I had to.

GAY DESIRE: Or else what?!

GAY IDENTITY: Or else we'd be extinct!

Beat. Acknowledging an impasse, GAY DESIRE *starts to slink away.*

GAY DESIRE: Well, that's enough truth for one night. You saved our lives, thank you . . . But the question remains: did you sell our souls to do it?

DEFYING DEFINITION, DEMANDING RECOGNITION: QUEER PERFORMANCE IN CANADA

LAINE HALPERN ZISMAN

To queer: to conceive, devour, dismantle, reproduce, cannibalize, and repeat. To be accountable to change and refuse stasis. To dream of being better.

Queer theatre communities are multiple, complex, layered, contradictory spaces of radical change, success, and failures. Our works are the product of power, abuse, erasures, oppressions, and instability (both from mainstream cis-het society and from within the confines of 2SLGBTQ+ creative spaces). Queer theatre creations are the stories of death and dying: A way to communicate and give name to the histories and present of intersecting genocides, exclusion, pandemics, epidemics, illness, love, joy, celebrations, and chosen and biological families. Queer theatre is how we make shelter from poetry and build homes in strange places, while addressing lived experiences of displacement, homelessness, violence, and danger. Queer theatres are the living room protests, uncomfortable crevices, back allies, and mainstages of grief, loss, and creation. The joy that comes from finding belonging and the narratives we construct when we cannot. Shattered and kaleidoscopic, we are forever moving, breaking, broken, and beautiful.

My own exposure to and understanding of 2SLGBTQ+ theatre is deeply embedded in my family histories and generations of ancestors who used theatre as a catalyst for systemic change. I learned through my mother, Shifra Brondel Zisman, a proud and out bisexual daughter of two survivors of genocide and refugees, that theatre and artistic practice are a means to imagine new possibilities. Queerness and bisexuality were interwoven into her artistic practice, a way to create, build, and sustain community. A member of Newfoundland Travelling Theatre Company, my mother taught me about the value of theatre as a *catalyst* for equity and justice, just as her father (my grandfather), Dovid Zisman—a playwright who was imprisoned in Buchenwald concentration camp—had taught her. "Cemeteries are exactly where we need to create theatre," my grandfather told my grandmother after their liberation. He used theatre to instigate a revolution, to ignite hope, to mourn the dead. My mother used theatre to explore identity, to find collectivity, to refuse definition, and to push boundaries. She used a stage name to mask her Jewish identity—from Shifra to Sheila—to escape antisemitism and find acceptance. Her Ashkenazi personhood and the murder of her grandparents, aunts, uncles, and cousins were hidden between letters of a pseudonym—the complexities of identities and closets. I learn from my grandfather and my mother how theatre can strengthen community *and* invisibilize histories. I take with me the power for art to simultaneously normalize oppression and uphold systemic inequities and at the same time to manifest change and create opportunities for 2SLGBTQ+ inclusion.

Queer theatre is how pasts are complicated and complicit, revolutionary, and regretful. Recognizing that what we think of as right and just today might require an apology tomorrow—queer theatre can refuse defensiveness and open its doors to learning. Queer theatre is collaboration and solitude.

At times, the queer theatre community can feel incredibly small, especially in the context of performance in Canada. In many ways, this can create a false assumption of a unified community, so that when we think of queer theatre, we think of one community, one style, one aesthetic. Too often this view of "queer theatre" becomes code for mainstream gay white theatre and excludes (or more often erases) works that do not fit within this category. But, despite what popular depictions and archives might seem to suggest, there is no *one* queer theatre community in Canada.

Historically, we can follow the success of queer theatre in Canada by marking some of the major theatre companies that create it. For example: Buddies in Bad Times Theatre (1979 to the present) in Toronto, Ontario, is the largest and longest running 2SLGBTQ+ theatre in the world; the frank theatre company (1996 to the present), is the oldest professional queer-mandated theatre company in Vancouver, British Columbia; Zee Zee Theatre has a mandated focus on 2SLGBTQ+ communities and recently launched a National Queer & Trans Playwriting Unit in partnership with nine other producing companies across Canada (2008 to the present); and Theatre Outré (2012 to the present), a professional queer theatre company based in Lethbridge, Alberta. However, while we should celebrate some of these companies' successes, it is also important to note that since their creation, much of their leadership and productions have centralized white and male gay voices. While more than a decade old, Jill Dolan's sentiment in *Theatre and Sexuality* still holds truth: "earlier views of the story of LGBTQ theatre in the USA, the UK, and elsewhere have focused almost exclusively on commercial theatre, where white men tend to be most visible and successful."* Indeed, in Canada gay cis-male performance often monopolized conversations about 2SLGBTQ+ theatre scholarship and practice in the past.

Indicative of this trend were conversations that transpired at the first national gathering of queer theatre and performance practice and scholarship in 2016, which was facilitated by Simon Fraser University and the frank theatre company in Vancouver, BC. The Q2Q Symposium was a central gathering space for previous and current 2SLGBTQ+ artistic directors, leading performance scholars, playwrights, and creators. With two subsequent publications that followed—one of performance texts and the other of scholarly reflection—the event was intended to unite a community across geographies. While its aims were valuable, the conversations that ensued were even more integral to the future of 2SLGBTQ+ performance in this country. The roundtables and dialogue throughout the gathering demonstrated the already (perhaps necessarily) fractured communities who create queer, trans, and gender expansive art. While the sessions were focused on "queer theatre to come" and queer theatre's past, the conversation moved quickly to unpack whose history the symposium was highlighting—what linear singular narrative was the gathering assuming the guests to share?

* Jill Dolan, *Theatre and Sexuality* vol. 31 (London: Bloomsbury Publishing, 2010), 5.

As Fay Nass reflected, much of the gathering "revolved around issues of race, culture, and the systematic effects of the ongoing colonization experienced by queer artists of colour."* With a distinctly intergenerational and racial divide, the conference represented a shift in consciousness for many cisgender and white settler practitioners in attendance who had narrowed the histories of queer and transgender performance in Canada.

Layers of grief, trauma, and communication barriers shaped days that were at once productive and detrimental to the future of queer and trans theatre and those who create it. Ultimately, the event made clear that by focusing primarily on a singular historical narrative of theatrical progress, the story of queer theatre and performance in Canada is narrowed and limited. This active *whitening* of history perpetuates, rather than troubles normative theatre narratives, upholding and strengthening white and settler colonial ideals and expectations of theatre and the arts. It is not simply that we need to elevate and support the works of non-binary and trans artists in the Global Majority, but we must remember and repair historical erasures of those artists creating in Canada throughout our pasts. In researching and elevating the works of Indigenous, trans, and non-binary performance in Canada we reveal the roots already securely at the foundation of our diverse histories.

Queer theatre is an invitation to recognize all the names and voices that have been erased, ignored, changed, or buried for too many reasons. Settlers, white individuals and organizations, cisgender people, those with class privilege, we all must recognize how space was and is allocated to those in positions of relative privilege—and of course, this does not erase shared or disparate queer and transgender struggles, but instead acknowledges the complexity of pain and oppression and the ways in which systemic violence and inequities shape each person's experiences differently.

Queer theatre invites calls for equity and change that move through and beyond gender and sexuality. Increasingly, queerness is not simply about

---

* Fay Nass, "Hybrid Between a Subjective and Critical Reflection on Q2Q: Symposium on Queer Theatre and Performance." *Canadian Theatre Review* 171 (2017): 107. https://doi.org/10.3138/ctr.171.018.

the intersections of our sexual orientation, gender, and sexuality but the need to be accountable to change, difference, and learning. Meaningful, equitable, and radical queer theatre is about communities and collectivities that are in a constant state of questioning and transformation.

Queer theatre is resurrection, re-creation, recalibration, and returns. It is a theatre that, out of necessity, must cannibalize itself, through a state of self-destruction that is reflexive of its own errors and critical of the power structures that it exists within. Queer theatre is messy and sexy and sad and hopeless and hopeful because existing in contradictions means we can refuse the borders of classifications and play through the fluidity of words and motions. Queer theatre is generous and demanding (because we deserve to demand). It is at times the product of vibrant cultures, new rituals, and well-worn traditions, and at others a suturing to white supremacy, settler colonialism, transphobia, and ableism. As much as queer and trans art pushes boundaries, sometimes it also reinforces them. Optimism risks erasures.

All queer theatre is not yet any or all the critical, just, and revolutionary aims we imagine, but perhaps we can breathe new lives and possibilities into fruition when we share what hopeful futures might bring. The stories we tell create and memorialize lived experience, boundless possibilities of futures untold, histories remembered, presents always in the making.

Dr. Laine Halpern Zisman is a post-doctoral fellow at the School of Public Health and Social Policy at the University of Victoria. Her research traverses the intersections of 2SLGBTQ+ equity, culture, and reproductive care. In addition to her scholarship in queer communications and culture, Halpern Zisman is a certified fertility support practitioner and family building educator, helping people navigate all stages of their perinatal journeys. She has published two collected volumes, Women and Popular Culture in Canada *(2020) and the second edition of* Queerly Canadian, *co-edited with Professor Scott Rayter (2023). Her third book focuses on 2SLGBTQ+ family building in Canada (Fernwood Publishing, forthcoming 2024).*

CHAPTER 5
EXPOSED

LAST SHOW ON EARTH TRADEMARK SYMBOL!

BRETON LALAMA

Breton Lalama (he + they) is a multi-medium artist committed to enriching and diversifying queer and trans representation in storytelling. He's a proud co-founder of the Spindle Films Foundation, an initiative created to support transgender Canadian filmmakers. They have been nominated for the Robert Merritt and Dora Mavor Moore Awards, and have won a BroadwayWorld and Tootsie Award. His play *The Last Show On Earth Trademark Symbol!* will premiere at Neptune Theatre in 2024. He is Tarragon Theatre's 2023 RBC Emerging Playwright in Residence. @bretonlikethecrackers.

The world is ending. Are you watching the livestream? With 201 days left till the end of the world, Eli works overtime at the Fruit Roll-Ups factory, trying to save enough to secure a black-market Fleedom Ticket to safety. But when a ghost from his past becomes the poster child of the apocalypse, things get a little bit sticky.

Ayo: any pronouns, any age, so long as we can feel they've lived a life. Loudly queer, androgynous former nightlife performer turned narrator of the apocalypse. Ayo is counting Earth down to the final day, when they'll headline *The Last Show On Earth Trademark Symbol!* Vices: attention, applause, adoration.

✦ WHEN YOU HURT SOMEONE ✦

AYO: When you hurt someone, you become a part of them.

You become something they carry around, the thing they think of when there's a sound in the night, and at a party when everyone's laughing, their mouths all big and full of teeth, you're the thing that they see at the back of the throat, you, just grinning, dangling from the uvula.

When you hurt someone, you get to become their truth.

It's a dirty way to live forever but it's a way.

It's such an easy thing to do. To hurt someone. You just have to press down on the place that's already bruised. There's always a bruise. Usually there are many. You could do it by accident. But I move with intention. I find the softest spot, run my palm over it, feel how you shiver just a little when I poke at it. How your eyes look away. I let you beg me.

To touch it. To not touch it.

And then

I

push. Hurt someone bad enough and you become immortal.

Or like, I hope so.

CULT PLAY

SCOUT REXE

Scout Rexe (they/she) is a playwright and dramaturge. As a writer, their work explores queer and trans identities, celebrity, sexual violence, and social change.

In *Cult Play*, Alex (thirties) has just escaped a cult masquerading as a progressive self-help group. Her girlfriend Taylor (thirties) remains indoctrinated by the cult and its charismatic leader Hunt (thirties). Alex is desperate to free Taylor before she becomes embroiled in fraud, sex trafficking, and murder. *Cult Play* is an investigation of the lure of community, what we will sacrifice for our beliefs, and how we try to save the people we love.

Alex (early thirties; a queer woman) has just arrived back from her first retreat at the Centre and her first time meeting Taylor—who she has been talking to online for a few months—in person. Alex has suspicions that the self-help group is cult-like, and that there are red flags around Taylor's behaviour, but she doesn't yet know the full extent of the cult or Taylor's role in it.

✦ SHE BREAKS UP WITH HER THERAPIST ✦

ALEX: Look, I know it sounds insane, I really do—I *get it*—but what I have with Taylor is, magic. It is.

Like when I got to The Centre I had lost my voice, but I'm always losing my voice. I thought it was because of my work—you know, we're always yelling in the kitchen. But when I saw her, she put her hand around my neck.

ALEX does this to herself, slowly, with her own hand.

And she said, "you don't have to do that anymore." You don't have to do that. She just held her hand there, and I started to cry because I knew, and she told me that I haven't been letting myself speak—I've been choking myself—and the strain of not *speaking*, you know, for *myself*, is literally making me lose my voice.

So then I got my voice back. I could speak perfectly fine the whole time I was there. Not one rasp.

Pause. ALEX is looking for a response.

I mean, *also*, the love-at-first-sight thing *is real*. I know you think it's woo-woo. But I know it's real—neuroscientists and other . . . experts have proven it. It's a real thing that happens in the brain, because of timing, and, and—mental schemas, you know? And there's an energy thing, too. *That's* real. Also proven.

She looks searchingly at her therapist, who reveals nothing.

And it's more than just love at first sight. Lots of people can feel that. It's, it's a Soul Mate Thing. I know lots of people don't believe in that; I get that it's a thing our culture *tells* us to believe. You know? From like, the nineteenth century. I know that. And I told myself a long time ago that none of this is real, it's all made up, it's all capitalism and just how we're organizing ourselves right now as humans.

But I feel it. I have it. I *have it.*

She starts to rush herself.

I just want to get it all out and then you can respond. I just don't want to lose it.

She exhales.

We were on FaceTime for three hours last night. She's still at The Centre. It looks so peaceful. Everything's so wet and lush and . . .

She inhales and exhales deeply.

The attraction is just . . . it's a drug. It's a drug. I'm high on the drug of her. And I don't want space. I've had space. I've had lonely. I've had reflecting and journaling and therapy and all that fucking shit that's supposed to heal you.

Healing can happen relationally, too. It's not just *being alone, in isolation* and doing fucking penitence for not being perfect.

She stares at him. It's a sort of challenge. He doesn't accept it.

I think it's just an attraction—it's a kind of attraction that I don't think you understand.

I don't mean because it's queer. I mean, I do think gay sex is better, but that's not what I'm trying to say. The connection—it just comes from such a deep sense of difference, of alienation, and even as we get older, and we have queer friends, or community, or whatever, there is this quiet sense in us—okay, in *me*, in me—this real loneliness, and then you find a connection with someone who *sees* you and they *love* you and they want to fuck you and bruise you and it's like, okay, here it is, I can be my full self, I can be known, I won't die alone. You know?

I don't know.

She looks like she's going to give up and then tries one last time.

I think because we're women, it all gets diminished. Like the intensity of the lust isn't a thing.

But it is.

It is. Even from a distance. Like last night I brought her to the bathroom with me because she wanted to watch me shower so I propped her up against a body wash and let her watch me turn in the water and we were both just so alive and turned on and and and *present* and from her little screen she said, "This is my teenage boy fantasy," and I ask what she's been fantasizing about and she says lots of penetration stuff and I brush my teeth and spit the toothpaste out slowly, to look like cum, which she loves.

Pause.

I know it's unreasonable, and we've known each other only for a few months, but those months have been big ones. I see her edges, too, and the way she acts out. I know why she pushes me away. My ego doesn't have to respond to that.

She told me not to worry. That she'll sabotage her self-sabotage before it happens.

She waits for her therapist to respond: a final test. He doesn't.

So I'm going to move there. I don't know why I'm not there now. I don't want to say that this weekly thing with you hasn't been helping, because it has. It brought me here. And I get that it fills such a huge gap, you know, without us having religious leaders anymore, like in the way we can trust, or that feels really sacred.

I just need something bigger than this. A way to live.

MOCKINGBIRD

ROB KEMPSON

Rob Kempson (he/him) is a theatre artist and educator, working largely as a director and playwright. His written work often investigates the impact of queerness in traditionally non-queer spaces, across myriad theatrical genres. He is the writer of The Graduation Plays (*SHANNON 10:40*, *Mockingbird*, *Trigonometry*), a trilogy of work navigating the complexity of sexuality in educational settings. He received a Dora Mavor Moore Award nomination for his musical, *The Way Back to Thursday* (Theatre Passe Muraille). Throughout his career, Rob has been fortunate to work with companies across the country, including the Stratford Festival, Shaw Festival, Young Peoples' Theatre, Sudbury Theatre Centre, Theatre Passe Muraille, Musical Stage Co., and the Thousand Islands Playhouse. In addition to his work as a playwright, Rob is the artistic director of the Capitol Theatre (Port Hope) and the co-artistic producer of ARC (with Deborah Drakeford). More info at robkempson.com or on Twitter/X at @rob_kempson.

When we first meet the English Department of Finch Park Collegiate, rumours are flying about a teacher-student relationship. Two days later, Mr. Foster has been removed from the school. With an eleven-person ensemble and razor-sharp dialogue, these teachers cast judgement on one another, make their own difficult choices, and share their worldview. *Mockingbird* reveals what happens when innocence meets authority, and explores the grey area between right and wrong. *Mockingbird* received its world premiere at the 2016 Next Stage Theatre Festival, playing to packed houses and unanimous acclaim. It broke box office records as the highest-revenue-generating show in Next Stage Theatre Festival history.

Zack is a student at Finch Park Collegiate. He technically graduated the year before but, after the death of his sister, came back for a fifth year to retake some courses and improve his marks before applying to university. Since the fall, he has been in a secret relationship with Mr. Foster—a teacher in the English department. This monologue comes at the end of the play when Zack confronts Ms. Lee, Mr. Foster's best friend and fellow teacher, about her role in the dissolution of his relationship.

Mockingbird was first produced by timeshare performance at Next Stage Theatre Festival in Toronto on January 6, 2016. It was performed by Tess Degenstein, Beau Dixon, Margaret Evans, James Graham, Stephen Jackman-Torkoff, Esther Jun, Andrew Moodie, Rahnuma Panthaky, Andrew Pimento, Kaitlyn Riordan, and Paula Wing; directed by Rob Kempson; with set and costume design by Brandon Kleiman; lighting design by Michelle Ramsay; sound design by Lyon Smith; stage management by Isabelle Ly; and produced by Lisa Li.

✦✦✦

ZACK confronts Ms. Lee in the staff workroom. He is wearing a very dirty homemade shirt that says "I Fucked Mr. Foster" on it.

ZACK: I can't believe you did this. You told him to break up with me.

I knew you would do this if he told you. But he said that you were his friend . . .

He's not picking up his phone, he's not responding to his texts, he deleted me from Facebook. All I want to do is talk to him. I went to his house and the lights weren't on.

But you didn't think about that, did you Miss Lee? We, like, bought stuff together. I know the kind of laundry detergent he uses. I know how he folds his socks just so. I know that he hates Teflon pans, and that he only eats bananas in the afternoon, and that he calls his mom on Monday nights because she has choir on Sundays. I know that he's been in dozens of failed relationships with men who are the "right" age. And this—this thing between us, this perfect thing—this apparently can't happen because I'm too young. Because of a fucking number . . .

I love him. I really really really love him. He means everything to me.

You know the school called my parents and told them that I'm a faggot. They TOLD them that I'm a faggot and that I was fucking Mr. Foster. They told them all of it. EVERYTHING. I came home and my dad hit me. My mom had packed a bag. I'm not allowed back in the house. I slept in the park last night.

Just like that. Just like that I'm homeless, and I don't know how long I can be homeless, you know? And I thought that I could just stay with him, just be with him, and that would make it all better. Because he doesn't even work at the school, right? But now I can't even do that.

I love him. And he loves me.

I know he does. I know I do. I'm not "too young" to know what that means, and he's not either because we're not stupid. We're in love. And now he's gone. And it's all your fault. It's all your fault. It's all YOUR FAULT!

Do you feel good now? That's what I want to know. Can you look me in the eyes and know that all of this has happened and tell me you feel good?

TERRIBLE WEATHER

COLLEEN MacISAAC

Colleen MacIsaac (they/them) is an interdisciplinary artist living in Mi'kma'ki (Halifax, Nova Scotia), working across theatre, drawing, illustration, video, graphic design, animation, comics, and performance. The artistic producer of the Villains Theatre, Colleen's recent performance creations include *A Beginner's Guide to the Night Sky*, *the effects were cumulative and i almost didn't notice*, *TO: THE UNKNOWN*, *Shortcuts*, *mercury*, *Cartography*, *The Blazing World*, and *dark matter*. They are a graduate of Emily Carr University (Bachelor of Media Arts in Animation) and NSCAD University (Master of Fine Arts in Studio, performance), and they have served on the boards of Theatre Nova Scotia, the Bus Stop Theatre Co-operative, and the Halifax Fringe Festival. A Robert Merritt Award nominee for Best Ensemble, Colleen is the winner of the Halifax Mayor's Award for Emerging Theatre Artist, the Bhayana Family Foundation "Invisible Champion" Award, and the Helen Hill Animated Award.

Terrible Weather is an interdisciplinary work that explores the effects of climate change on our mental health.

After the storm, we remember what happened.

✦ AFTER THE STORM ✦

WE: After the storm, after the trees lay heavily, their tiniest branches still, still in the dead air, after our home was gone, flattened under the spruce and the birch and the aspen, after the high dark sky loomed again, its distance more crushing than ever before, after the storm is when I kissed you and told you that our time was coming to an end.

That's not how it happened. It happened like this: After the storm, after the sea had dissipated, leaving scattered branches in its wake, after the blood had stopped flowing freely from the wounds, after the old pines had finished their wailing and the clouds grew pale from the sight, after the storm is when I kissed you and told you that all was not lost.

That's not how it happened. It happened like this: After the storm we held hands and hoped the night would hold off. We spent hours searching through splinters, we cleared paths, we sought water that we could drink, water that was clean, water that ran clear. On the horizon we could see a strange dark line. I whispered to you that more storms were coming, there was nothing we could do.

It happened like this: After the storm you helped me walk to the water's edge, and we sat there together, huddled, shivering, the trees terribly still behind us. I searched through the debris next to us. Silence blanketed the dead sky, and I whispered to you that help would come soon, it must be coming soon.

It happened like this: You found a feather and I started weeping and couldn't stop. There was no wind. You found a stone shaped like a small flat coin. You found a bottle of fresh water.

That sounds about right. I found a feather.

I found a feather, and we heard, far off through the silence, the cry of some strange bird.

And I kissed you, and we said nothing.

And I kissed you back, and we said nothing.

A DRUNK LESBIAN LOVE AFFAIR

THALÍA GONZÁLEZ KANE

Thalía González Kane (she/her) is an award-winning, queer, Ecuadorian Canadian multidisciplinary artist. She has worked as a performer, voice-over artist, playwright, director, designer, composer, choreographer, and producer in Canada, England, Ireland, Scotland, Sweden, Czechia, and various states in the USA. Thalía is a co-founder of Got Your Back Canada, co-chair of outACTRAto, and the artistic director of Crave Productions. She has been published by University of Toronto Press, *Intermission Magazine*, and *Canadian Theatre Review*. Thalía was named a playwright to watch by Playbill in 2020 for her show *A Drunk Lesbian Love Affair*. The play was also a finalist for the Oscar Wilde Prize for Best New Writing in Dublin, Ireland.

"The fact is that I love you. I am drunk. And I love you." They're young. They're drunk. They're in love . . . until they sober up. *A Drunk Lesbian Love Affair* chronicles the escapades of Sally and her "drunk lesbian lover" through a haze of whiskey and wine. This one-person show explores the vulnerability of love, our relationships and sexuality, queerness, and coming into one's own. A tender-hearted comedy, *A Drunk Lesbian Love Affair* combines millennial discourse, poeticism, and movement in the search for a sober love.

Sally is a queer cis-woman in her mid-twenties. She hasn't quite figured out what she wants from life yet, but she lives it boldly anyway. She bounces between jobs and has the spirit of an artist. She is an old soul and an absolute romantic—but she tries not to let it show. Note that her attempts are rarely successful. She has a heart of gold and the best of intentions, but in the end, is only human.

A Drunk Lesbian Love Affair was first produced at the International Dublin Gay Theatre Festival, Dublin, Ireland, on May 6, 2019. It was performed by Thalía González Kane, directed by Eimear Keating, with stage management and design by Lisa Barry.

✦✦✦

SALLY: So, we were at a movie.
A film with someone famous in it.
Part of a festival.
We think we're classy because we go out to the cinema in this day of Netflix and chill.
So fucking civilized.
The movie was fine, I think.
I sat to her left with my hand on the armrest between us.
Midway through I feel her hand reach out and hold mine.

We're just friends.

But she's holding my hand.
During the day.
In a public place.
But in a dark theatre, it almost feels like anything goes.

I slip my fingers through hers and hold her hand so tightly.
Each of us pulsing back and forth to each other, the way you do.
It's so small but so intimate and so perfect and I forget what happened in the rest of the movie because I played that scene with her and I in my head over and over until the film ended and we clapped and we left.

Exiting the theatre, we pushed though the crowds and she led the way, taking my hand, again.
We emerged at the other end and I look at her with this dumb smile she knows all too well.
I have to go and she leans in to kiss my cheek.
I ask to see her later.
She says maybe.

A few hours later she called me.
Invited me over.
We drank wine together and got Thai take out.
We wonder why we never have any savings.
Whatever.
What's cool about this relationship is that it's not.
Like, it's not a real relationship.
We can go out and drink and laugh and forget about all the garbage in our lives.
And everything seems fine.
Sure, we flirt.
And sometimes we dance.

Bumping lights and music rise. She dances through the remainder of the scene.

Sometimes I kiss her neck—if it feels appropriate.
And then her hand does this thing where it slips to my lower back.
That could be anybody though.

But tonight, I am gonna go home.
ALONE.
Because I am in control.

All the feelings I have, I want.

I am the fucking master of my feelings. And I don't want her.

Music starts rising.

I am in CONTROL.

She pulls out her cellphone and begins texting. We know who she is messaging. She dances herself into oblivion.

A ROOM FACING SOUTH

GORDON PORTMAN

Gordon Portman (he/they) has worked as playwright/librettist, dramaturge, teacher, producer, actor, and director in theatres, rehearsal halls, and classrooms from Victoria to Halifax. His award-winning work as a playwright has been featured at the Blyth Festival and Port Hope Festival Theatre in Ontario; at Fringe Festivals in Winnipeg and Edmonton; at SummerWorks in Toronto; and in Saskatoon, where in the fall of 2022, Live Five and Pegasus Productions staged the world premiere of his latest full-length play, *After Sundown*, in which a genderfluid child returns to the difficult home of their origin to help take care of a parent afflicted with Alzheimer's. Gordon is also an actor, dramaturge, director, teacher, and producer, and has recently completed an M.A. in Theatre Theory and Dramaturgy through the University of Ottawa.

Brett Holland is a middle-aged, cis gay male—an outspoken, playwright/activist turned academic, somewhat afraid that his voice is no longer heard and/or relevant. His research into gay novelist E.M. Forster leads him into contact with Daniel Khan, a genderqueer archivist. There is sexual tension between the two, but there is also conflict as the educated but somewhat flighty Daniel is uninformed about 2SLGBTQ+ history, and dismissive of the activism of which Brett was a part. As their flirtation deepens and as Brett conducts his research, time and reality bend as Brett interacts with the Forster brought to life by Brett's imagination. As his potential relationship with Daniel falls apart, Brett completes his academic investigations, unapologetic and confrontational, determined to keep fighting for truths he believes the world is still far from living.

As the play begins, Brett arrives at Cambridge University in England to begin his research. He encounters Daniel, who challenges Brett's colonialist perspectives even as the two explore their mutual attraction. Their banter is simultaneously playful, intellectual, and confrontational, as Daniel's perceptive comments puncture Brett's self-importance. Finally, while they are sharing a flirtatious picnic, Brett explodes.

✦✦✦

BRETT: It's a good thing you're pretty because, baby, there's a big part of you that's missing—no no no, Oprah, you are NOT perfect as you are because, you see, the thing about queerness—which is the story of queer art, which is the story of you, because you're the product of that history and that art, and the story of me because I'm part of that history, even if you think I and my art are fucking "over" . . . ! The thing is that for centuries, for CENTURIES, we lived in, and we defined, for us and for everyone like us, the age and the art of metaphor. WE were metaphor. We LIVED it. We disguised ourselves as them. In art and life. Metaphor as closet, and vice versa, which means, my lovely, that you have Michelangelo, while he was painting the Sistine Chapel, showing the poor slobs on their knees before a God that looked exactly, exactly like the "Hot Daddy Threesome" guy I saw on Grindr yesterday—the abs, the beard, the bulging towel—and let me tell you that is not Adam's finger he was really reaching for—which the pope knew, because he was diddling the cardinals, and which the cardinals knew because they were diddling the choirboys—but which the choirboys didn't know, actually; all they knew was that their mothers could put food on the table. The age of metaphor defined our art for centuries, which ultimately means it defined all art because we are the tribe of art, the tribe of seeing beneath things, the meaning beneath things, because we have LIVED beneath. Beneath the veil. And some would say beneath the rock, but here's another thing—underneath the rock, underneath the darkness, it's where the seeds grow. They know the sun is there to find, and that they have as much right to that light and that joy and that living . . . ! And they reach. And they grow. And they, and we, we fucking dance. But then you get the mid-eighteen hundreds, your Walt Whitmans, your Herman Melvilles, your Nathaniel Hawthornes, the veil starts to get a little thinner—you get to the early mid-nineteen hundreds and you get to your Gertrude Steins, your Noël Cowards, your Terrence Rattigans, your fucking Oscar Wildes, and all the metaphor, all the gay reality masquerading as the longings and frustrations, mostly of women, in their corsets and their desperation, their repression and their slamming doors, the living outside, the living beneath—all of it, ALL of it, the ages and ages of metaphor, but the veils are getting thinner and thinner, and THEN you get to 1949. Edward Morgan Forster, known to friends and family as Morgan. Closet case and mama's boy—the two are not unrelated. Lover of all things Italian, Indian, and uncut. Has a lot of early success when he's very young and is very pleased with himself, and in 1924, after he publishes *A Passage to India*, a lot of other people are very pleased with him and are really looking forward to what's coming next, but there is nothing for more than twenty years. Nothing. Not even *Maurice*, his hope for "a happier time" where two men could love each other freely and safely—with the safest possible sex you can imagine, i.e., COMPLETELY inhibited, but still, you know, naked together—he sat on that novel, that dream, for decades, DECADES, never mind how many sanities he could've saved, never mind how many lives—I'm only a little bitter—I mean come on, there's a depression, there's a war, there's Nazis and Fascism and slaughter—you should look that up some time—but the man who passionately believes that a room with the right kind of view could change a life, literally and metaphorically, pisses around with essays and letters and a diary in which he spends most of his time moaning about not having enough time with his married policeman boyfriend and keeps his dreams for the human race to himself. BUT! In 1949, he turns seventy years old. In 1949, he decides to work on the text for an opera, something he has never done before. That opera is based on a short novel by Herman Melville called *Billy Budd*, one of the most homoerotic short stories in literature. That opera is being composed by Benjamin Britten, who just happens to be one of the few faggots in England who was both relatively out and happily partnered. That opera is the story of a beautiful man who embodies goodness, and compassion, and joy, and in 1949, when Morgan Forster's spent his entire life so far in the closet he can't see daylight—! He decides he needs to be part of a retelling of that story. AND! Or perhaps so, we don't know—! In 1949, Morgan Forster, British to the core of his bad teeth and sexual repression; Morgan Forster, Victorian-born, Edwardian-raised, and Empire-bred, turns down a knighthood! Maybe because working on *Billy Budd* was a cracking open of the closet door, his closet door, our closet door—starting to let his stories, our stories, out for air, and light, and tomorrows. This is because Billy Budd, in the original, is beautiful, both physically and morally, and it's metaphor, again, and still, for men loving men—it's all behind the veil, that truth that Morgan Forster wanted to be his truth. BUT! The veil is pretty trans-fucking-parent—and the pun is completely intended. THEN! In the original and in the opera, Vere and Claggart, Billy's captain and the master-at-arms—Billy is a sailor—these two manly men, testicles clanking, they hate the male goodness and the male beauty—Billy's truth, and Melville's truth, and Forster's truth, and Britten's truth, and mine, and yours! Claggart attacks Billy, Billy kills him in self-defense, Vere sees to it that Billy's hanged for mutiny, Billy forgives him just before he dies, and Vere survives to be a closet case another day, and there you have the seeds of almost every dead queer narrative to the present *day*. But it's a step, a step away, or out, or more. Time marches on—it dances on. The less said about the fifties the better, unless you're talking Audrey Hepburn, Douglas Sirk, and *All About Eve* and *Sunset Boulevard*, and then all bets are off. But you get to the sixties, and the seventies, and you get all KINDS of voices ripping through all kinds of veils. You have the James Baldwins and the Malcolm xs and the Angela Davises, you have the Germaine Greers and the Simone de Beauvoirs and the Gloria Steinems, you have the Leslie Silkos and the Scott Momadays and then for us you have the faggot writers like Alan Hollinghurst and bell hooks and me, me, and Tony Kushner and Paula Vogel, all of us pushing aside the whiteness and the straightness and the patriarchy and the masculinity because we need the veils gone and because we are DONE, we're done with the back of the bus, baby! We can paint the bus pink! And we can FUCK in the bus—and that is NOT metaphor—well it is, but it's not, because the fucking is the reason for the big old pride parade we started, all around the world—I mean the goddamn ROMANS, with the Bacchus and the Bacchanalia and the breaking the rules, and all of it associated with fucking—? That's the reason straight people hate us more than ANYTHING because fucking is FREEDOM, a freedom we have that they do not—in the bus, or on the beach, the bedroom or the basement of my father's church, which I did once and it was HOT! The fucking and the fuck you—? It's at the heart of all the male faggots, female faggots, faggots in between—it's at the heart of all of us because all faggots, ALL faggots, are hated, somewhere—everywhere!—and it is the heart of you because in spite of everything you have, and everything you are, and everything you're free to claim, you are still someone who someone else, somewhere, wants to kill, without knowing anything about you, other than you want to fuck someone that capitalism, patriarchy, and Christianity—not that there's a lot of difference between the three of them—someone that they all think you shouldn't be able to fuck, or love, or marry, or even fucking know are THERE! So we keep dancing, we keep fucking, and we keep fighting. For real. Not metaphor. NOT metaphor. And we are never, EVER done, so do NOT tell me I am over! I made you possible—WE made you possible and do not ever EVER forget it!

THE AFTERPARTY

ELIZABETH STAPLES AND JORDAN CAMPBELL

We are a performer-director duo called Jord and Liz. Jordan (any pronoun) is a queer performer, dancer, theatre artist, and party maker. Also known as STARLIGHT, she throws queer parties in Toronto like WISHING WELL and Magic Chicks! Jordan is half of xLq POP ART Performance (with Maddie Bautista), and he is the artistic director of the neurodiverse theatre company the Purple Stage. Elizabeth (Liz) Staples (she/her) is a bi/queer settler of Italian ancestry who was born and raised in Tkarón:to (Toronto). She is a multidisciplinary theatre creator, performance artist, director, and arts administrator. Together, Jord and Liz have been collaborating for over eight years on various theatre and dance projects, parties, and site-specific performances. From 2020 to 2022, we created outdoor performance journeys and drag shows using a silent disco system: *The Afterparty* and *PARTYPEOPLE*. Jord and Liz make spaces to imagine the future of queer gathering.

In *The Afterparty*, STARLIGHT invites you to a site-specific performance-art drag experience for a single audience member that's physically distant yet socially intimate. Meet her in the park, listen to the soundtrack through your headphones, and be prepared to be taken on an interactive journey through a music video-esque experience of pop music, costume reveals, meditations, questions, and choices. It's a cinematic exploration of nature, intimacy, and public queerness.

This monologue was a part of the performance track for *The Afterparty*. A cosmic club kid witch from beyond called STARLIGHT has joined a single audience member in the park. They have just danced really hard together. STARLIGHT is deciding how to move forward by looking back. She asks the audience for help choosing an outfit.

The Afterparty was first developed at Buddies in Bad Times Theatre's Pride in Place Festival, Toronto, in June 2020. It was first performed in September 2020 as part of the Bricks and Glitter Festival in Toronto. It was performed by Jordan Campbell (STARLIGHT), directed by Elizabeth Staples, with stage management by Robin Gaudreau.

✦ SWEATY ✦

STARLIGHT: I'm sweaty.
Do you love me?
Can you see the past?
It's fading
It's raining
It looks like rain.
It looks like rain.

I'd rather be dry but . . .
at least I'm alive.

I saw you in the park
Our eyes met.
There was music.
We danced.
You looked beautiful.

But nothing lasts forever.
It's time for you to choose.

This dress or this dress?
This wig or this wig?
These glasses or these glasses?
This jacket or this jacket?
This ring or this necklace?

Are you happy with these choices?
Do you want to keep going or do you want to go home?

Take a deep breath.
Look around.
Are you the only one here?
Are you the only one queer?

Look at the trees.
Look at the sky.
This is our revolution.
Look at your feet on the ground.
This is our dance floor we fought for.

Now close your eyes.
This is when it starts.
Open your eyes.
LOOK. AT. ME. NOW.

STREET OF BLOOD

RONNIE BURKETT

Ronnie Burkett (he/him) has been captivated by puppetry since the age of seven and began touring his shows around Alberta at the age of fourteen. Ronnie Burkett Theatre of Marionettes was formed in 1986, continuously playing on Canada's major stages and as a guest company on numerous tours abroad. Ronnie has received the 2009 Siminovitch Prize in Theatre, the Herbert Whittaker/CTCA Award for Distinguished Contribution to Canadian Theatre, a *Village Voice* OBIE Award, and four Citations of Excellence from the American Center of the Union Internationale de la Marionnette. In 2019, Ronnie Burkett was appointed as an Officer of the Order of Canada. *Forget Me Not* is the fourteenth production from Ronnie Burkett Theatre of Marionettes, following the international successes *Penny Plain*, *Billy Twinkle*, *10 Days on Earth*, *Provenance*, and the Memory Dress Trilogy of *Tinka's New Dress*, *Street of Blood*, and *Happy*. *The Daisy Theatre*, Ronnie's wildly popular and ever-changing marionette vaudeville show, and the Daisy Christmas show, *Little Dickens*, continue touring to great acclaim. Ronnie lives in Toronto, and from his studio (known in puppetry circles as Puppetland) he continues to imagine and create new work.

When Mrs. Edna Rural pricks her finger and bleeds onto her sewing, she sees the face of Christ in a quilt square. As the media and the faithful converge on her sleepy prairie town, a has-been Hollywood vampire seeking rejuvenation and a karaoke-singing gay terrorist intent on revenge join the fray. And just as the bloodbath begins, the man in the quilt appears in the flesh to the odd trio, revealing that the bonds of blood are thicker and stranger than their individual thirsts led them to believe.

Street of Blood was first produced by Rink-A-Dink Inc./Ronnie Burkett Theatre of Marionettes at the Manitoba Theatre Centre, Winnipeg, in April 1998. It was performed by Ronnie Burkett; with music and sound design by Cathy Nosaty; lighting design by Bill Williams; stage management by Terri Gillis; and marionette, costume, and set design by Ronnie Burkett.

✦✦✦

EDEN: For six years I lived with the nicest man. Anthony. Eden and Anthony. We were the perfect couple. Everyone told us so. I was in love. Once. A long time ago. But it was brutal. It wasn't Anthony, although I grew to be afraid of him too.

See, Anthony looked like a gay icon. Like those perfect, ridiculous, empty men in underwear ads. V-shaped, hairless, air-brushed. And that's really fucking hard to be around, man, because it caused me to look at myself a considerable amount more than I prefer. Who can look that much sadness and anger in the face? Not me. Not when it's mine. But we had everything. Except passion. And besides, I couldn't leave him. We had too much stuff.

One Saturday afternoon I was lying on the couch while Anthony was in the basement working out. And there on TV was my sign—my epiphany—in the form of an old Esmé Massengill movie, *No Room For Love*, in which she played Constance Hart, a wealthy society dame married to an abusive banker who forfeits comfort and home and social standing to run off with a long-haul trucker named Butch, played brilliantly by Armand Collier. Butch. Oh hump-daddy Butch. That guy was as dangerous as day-old sushi.

Once again, Esmé came through for me! She was my inspiration. Fuck the house. Screw the stuff. Okay, so I didn't have a long-haul trucker waiting for me, but I had a car. A 1986 powder blue Monte Carlo. I got up off that couch and packed. Favourite clothes, photo albums, some books, my pipe bomb stuff, the duvet and two pillows, all the CDs that were mine, a boom box, and almost anything that was battery operated. And the cellphone. I was on the run, true, but I still needed access to my voice mail. Into the car it went. I had found my new home. And my escape. It was decided and done, start to finish, in thirty-five minutes.

Thirty-five minutes. It took six years to build something, to accumulate all the trappings, and thirty-five minutes to end it. But then, destruction is always quicker than creation. And way more noticeable.

I went downstairs to tell Anthony I was leaving. "Keep the house, keep everything, I have to go. I can't stay here anymore. I can't stay with you." And he started to cry. Well, I like to think they were tears, not just sweat running down his face. Eventually, he spoke. "It's because I bore you, isn't it?"

Of course I lied. I said no.

And left. But lemme tell ya, life isn't like the movies. In *No Room For Love*, just as Constance and Butch finally hit the road, they both die when the truck skids off a bridge in the rain. My fate was worse. I lived.

SHE'S JUST AS SCARED OF YOU AS YOU ARE OF HER

LIOR MAHARJAN

I've been relating to a spider lately. Imagine dancing with those legs? Not a special spider or anything. Something common. Something you'd find indoors. Something that you might face as a dilemma: to evict, under a glass, into the streets; or squash her. And while calmly spinning a web to catch tasty skeeters, totally unaware of how she might be inspiring brutality in the humans around her, the spider might wonder: "What am I trying to be?"

Back in the days when you were being socialized as a little boy, you loved wearing heels and dresses, wrapping a headscarf like long flowing hair, and stuffing a pillow under your shirt. Not in a cliché trans girl way, though. I mean, yeah, it was partially about feeling pretty, but (I think more importantly) it was about feeling special. For Halloweens and school plays to come, it wasn't rare to get a sighting of you all dolled up—in costume as a princess, popstar, or grandma. It felt exhilarating to lean into your femininity on these occasions when stepping out of everyday norms was welcome. And it's cool that this behaviour was tolerated in your childhood. And it's not like *not* putting makeup on ever stopped anyone from calling you a he-she either.

You still like getting dolled up. You want to feel hot for your friends, your world. Whether on stage or off, you want to look good, and if the character is not supposed to be looking good then you somehow find a way to look not good in a hot way. Cute and ill. Enchantingly disgusting. Going out, you feel much more confident after having put an unseemly amount of time into getting ready—again, not a cliché because you, love, are not a cliché. You're just slow and you know that nothing's sweeter than the birth of a fire fit. Donning armour to stun. Maybe you take your time getting ready just to delay the confronting eyes of strangers. Spectators that you want to believe have the potential to be strong supporting characters in your narrative, but chances are likely won't. Sometimes they're ladies, sometimes they're children, most often they're men. Sometimes they give looks of interest, of apathy, of disgust. Sometimes they're neighbours, sometimes they're also visibly queer, and sometimes they follow you in their dark Honda as you bike home at night. They're not the ones you dressed for, they're not the people you're out to see. They're just bodies between points A and B. And once the adrenaline that coursed—as you locked up your bike, as he pulled over, as you fumbled your keys while running up the stairs, as he approached your closing door—has subsided, you wonder: "What to do with all this attention that I can neither consent to nor withhold consent from?"

Writing started out as an outlet for you to explore gender's complexity. Ahem—cliché. And you write plays! It's been a while, though. You haven't felt very compelled to make action out of words lately. The last script you birthed was tough. Sure, the gestation was fulfilling—adapting a book you love into a stage play over the course of a few years—but production left you emptied. Iffy labour practices, unsavoury interactions, incongruent politics, and poor pay: delivering this show that you love took its toll. And the theatre didn't even make any efforts toward financial accessibility at the box office for the often marginalized and disenfranchised audiences that you wrote this play for. It left you demoralized. You wonder if you can trust producers. You wonder if you can trust your own capacity to produce. You don't know, so instead of knowing or writing, for now, you're translating and performing the words of others. Ain't that nice? For once, not feeling that pressing need to draft something original in response to the world.

You recently performed in a queer show with a bunch of cool, independent, interdisciplinary artist-friends. It was a gig that, in many ways, fulfilled. Time and money were limited but you felt that camaraderie was propelling the process despite the finite resources. It's a sad cliché in the industry—and yes, I agree: enough with the clichés! Got it. Anyway, it wasn't necessarily an easy process. It was actually a very tough show to do. Many challenges, many obstacles, and you craved support. There were times when you needed care and care was offered, and sometimes care was offered with kindness but it wasn't the kind of care you desired and you had trouble expressing that you needed something different, and sometimes others didn't have the capacity to offer care at a given moment and you had to care for yourself. Sometimes you were able to rise to the occasion and offer someone care and it was received with expressed gratitude and care was, in turn, returned. Other times, you tried but faltered, misread a signal, didn't offer the care that someone you care for needed. This project you love is also one that tested your faculties. It's an all-too-familiar image—artistic glory painted bloody and bruised. And you can accept the nuances of these things but still you wonder: "Can I really find a 100 per cent harm-free way to do shit?"

You smashed your chin open biking home from the theatre a few weeks back. You had contemplated walking your bike home, it was only twenty minutes by foot and you had big bags. The thought of your bed coerced you onto your bike and within five seconds of peddling off, your shoulder bag slipped down your arm, jammed into the front wheel, and you were sent flying over the handlebars. Landing on the asphalt chin first, your legs curled back above you, you no longer resembled a spider, but a giant scorpion making love to a bicycle. Kind strangers helped you to your feet, disentangled you from the bike, accompanied you home, and didn't call you "ladyboy," or chase you. The adrenaline walked home alongside you too. Your partner cleaned you up as you avoided looking in the mirror, before informing you that it was deep enough to need stitches and that you should definitely go to the ER. So, you make your way to the hospital, grateful that you just barely smashed the money-maker. Blood oozing down your neck as you ride the metro, people side-eye you, not as scared of you as you are of them, but seemingly disturbed and you couldn't care less. Your chin throbs as you reflect on this near-death experience. You could have bit your tongue off or broken some teeth, gotten a concussion, or far, far worse, but you're alive. Still unsure of what you're trying to be or what you should try to be, you wonder: "Is there anything out there truly strong enough to squash me and, if there is, can we be friends?"

Lior Maharjan is a Tiohtiá:ke-based writer/actor. Writing primarily for the stage and screen, they've taken on commissions for original scripts, adaptations, and translations. Their play From the Stars in the Sky to the Fish in the Sea *received eight nominations at the 2022 Montreal English Theatre Awards, including for Outstanding New Text and Production. As an actor, Lior's solo performance of Wajdi Mouawad's* Alphonse *at the 2022 Edinburgh Festival Fringe received critical acclaim. They appear in Mattias Graham's recent short film,* Bleach, *and provide voiceover on Netflix and Ubisoft projects. Lior co-founded bigT collective, which develops trans-centric theatrical and virtual creations. Their work entails producing, directing, consulting, modelling, dubbing, mentoring, facilitating, adjudicating grants, providing dramaturgy, and serving on boards, but never all at the same time.*

CHAPTER 6
TOUCH BUT DON'T TELL

FLUID

NICK MAYNARD

Nick Maynard (he/him) is a queer writer and artist living in Manchester, England. His work has been performed all over the UK and the US, and in 2017 it was showcased at the first LGBTQ festival in Sligo, Northern Ireland. Last year his play *Quaranteen* won the V International Playwriting Contest for plays for young audiences, and is being translated and published in Spanish by Editorial DALYA. His first novel, *Cripple*, is now available to buy from Amazon.

This is a self-contained monologue about a young man whose sexuality is best described as fluid.

Fluid has been performed at the Southwark Playhouse as part of Director's Cut (2017); the Royal Exchange as part of Mother's Ruin (2017); the Hen and Chickens Theatre Bar, Islington, as part of Full Disclosure's Xposure (2017); and the Lowry and Hope Mill Theatre in Manchester by Green Carnation Company as part of OutStageUs (2019) and the Queer All About It, part of Turn On Fest (2021).

✦✦✦

A YOUNG MALE *between fifteen and twenty-five years old enters. He is dressed in streetwear and appears to be "thuggish"—not the sort of lad you'd expect to be contributing to a night like this. He enters with a shy bravado—slightly fidgety and unsure of how to act. He is carrying a microphone—one presumes this is to be used in his "act." He looks like a rapper.*

YOUNG MALE: *(through the microphone to the audience)* Yo! Yo! Yo! Fuck! Ye'!

So— They think I'm gunna do this rap-thing about how fuckin' shit it is to grow up in Bolton, right? But I'm not! People like me don't get places like this to speak in, you know what I mean? Where people have to just sit there and listen. So, I'm gunna proper speak.

The YOUNG MALE *notices something in the wings. It's the organizers of the event, who are about to pull the plug on him.*

(to the people in the wings) Don't you fuckin' dare!

The YOUNG MALE *picks up a chair that is on the stage and throws it into the wings.*

I swear down, if you try to stop me some cunt's gunna get fuckin' hurt—you get me? Good. Now back the fuck off . . .

We get the sense that they have "backed the fuck off."

(to the audience) See . . . *(the microphone doesn't work anymore)* See—this is what I'm talkin' about. They just proper wanna keep shuttin' you down all the time. My mam's here—out there in the dark somewhere—can't

see her . . . There she is. All right! My brother—girlfriend—a few mates. Stevo! And they're all dead made up that I got this chance to be here. My mam said people like us don't get opportunities like this, and you have to grab them with both hands. Stevo thinks I'm gunna be the next fuckin' Professor Green or somethin'. Fuckin' dick. Gemma—I love you—you know that—but I have to do this. Stevo. Mam. I'm sorry. They think I'm proper brave standin' up here—but I'm not. I'm a coward. I can only do this because you're in the dark and I can't see you—and you can't answer me back. It's like safety in numbers, innit. All these people.

Right! Okay! I'm gunna say it. Shit! I practised this in my bedroom—my stomach's fuckin' proper churnin' man. *(grabbing at his crotch)* And my fuckin' balls have fuckin' gone. Fuck! This is scary.

I know what you all think. You think I'm gunna tell you that I'm gay or some bullshit like that, innit. Well, I'm not. If I was gay it would be easier, I swear down. I'm straight—but I do fuck guys. I'm not bi or anything . . . It's girls that I like in that way—but it's lads that I fuck. I'm not a rent boy or anything. I don't do it for money. I don't fuckin' know why I do it. I just do. And that's it. I know you probably think I'm some sort of messed up little queer or somethin'. That I've got *(parodying the middle classes) "fuckin' issues"*— Well I haven't. I know what I am. One-hundred per cent red-blooded male—and proper straight as a fuckin' die. I know that because I don't fancy them—not in that way. I don't have any problem with gays—some of the lads I fuck are probably gay. But most aren't. You haven't got a fuckin' clue about what I'm talkin' about, have you? I can see it in your eyes. You think you do. You think it's me that doesn't know what he's talkin' about. That if I fuck a lad, I must be gay. But it doesn't work like that. Things are different now. It's like if I was choosin' someone for fuckin' football or somethin'—you don't choose someone because you fancy them—you choose them because they play well, and that's why you want them to be part of your team. It's like a fuckin' match. A physical thing, where you get a hard-on and fuck—and while I'm fuckin' him I don't think about whether I love him or not—I just want to fuckin' own him—be inside him—be part of him. It's like a fuckin' sport. A fight. It's the fuckin' hardness of his body. The fuckin' muscle and the tendons of him—the fuckin' hardness—the sweaty fuckin' hardness of fuckin' him. Hard skin and bone. Violent. Vicious. Aggressive. You get me? You could do what we do with a girl. You wouldn't do what we do with a girl. You couldn't. What I do to him is different. There's a difference between love and what I do with him. It's all blood, and spit, and piss, and shit, and cum, and when I think of it I get so fuckin' hard I could fuckin' cum right now, I swear down.

I fuck in a fleetin' world beyond gender—beyond fuckin' gay or straight, good and evil, moral or immoral. What I am is part of a *"next generation"* who fuckin' engineer their own sexuality, in a world where sex and morality are more fluid than you could ever fuckin' imagine! Where who you fuck and how you fuck has no boundaries and no fuckin' rules—beyond the limitations of labels. Sexuality is transitory. Irrelevant. I'm evolvin' as a human being by explorin' new sexual realities. I celebrate my fuckin' gender by fuckin' my gender. I get hard at the perfection of a toned, sinewed body. I cum because of how it feels when fuck it. I'm not gay—I'm straight—and I fuck lads because I fuckin' can!

The YOUNG MALE *singles out another young male in the audience and makes meaningful eye contact with him.*

(while retaining intense eye contact) And that's all I wanted to say.

There is a thought and an intention that lingers on the YOUNG MALE*'s face before he turns and leaves the stage with a swagger.*

POLY QUEER LOVE BALLAD

ANAIS WEST AND SARA VICKRUCK

Anais West (they/he) is a queer, trans writer, actor, and producer. They are also a Polish settler based on occupied xʷməθkʷəy̓əm (Musqueam), Sḵwx̱wú7mesh (Squamish), and səlil̓wətaʔɬ (Tsleil-Waututh) lands. Anais's work is interdisciplinary, merging theatre, film, music, and poetry to explore the multiplicity within gender, sexuality, culture, and self. Anais's writing includes *The Café* (ITSAZOO, Aphotic Theatre, and the PuSh Festival, Vancouver), the short theatrical film *Underground Absolute Fiction* (Rumble Theatre's Tremors Festival), the video-play hybrid *Kill Your Lovers* (Buddies in Bad Times Theatre's Rhubarb Festival, Tkarón:to, and the Fresh Fruit Festival, NYC), and the slam poetry musical *Poly Queer Love Ballad* (Queer Arts Festival, the frank theatre company, and Zee Zee Theatre, Vancouver, and Theatre Passe Muraille, Tkarón:to). Anais was awarded PTC's 2018 Fringe New Play Prize as well as first place in the 2023 Wildfire National Playwriting Competition. They've been nominated for two Jessie Richardson Awards, including Outstanding Original Script. As an actor, they've worked with Firehall Arts Centre, Savage Society, Théâtre La Seizième, Orange Noyée, the National Arts Centre, and more. Anais is the artistic producer at the frank theatre company.

Sara Vickruck (they/their) is an award-winning queer performer and theatre creator living in Vancouver, Canada. Born and raised in Alberta, Sara moved to Vancouver to continue growing their career in music and acting. They self-produced their debut album *Prologue* in 2015. Their most recent theatre credits include *Peace Country* (rice & beans theatre), *Romeo and Juliet* (Bard on the Beach), *Talking Sex on Sundays* (Firehall Arts Centre), *Coriolanus* (Bard on the Beach), *Fun Home* (Arts Club Theatre Company), *Circle Game* (Firehall Arts Centre), *West Side Story* (Theatre Under The Stars), *Kill Your Lovers* (Buddies in Bad Time's Rhubarb Festival), and *Love Bomb* (Shameless Hussy Productions), for which they won an OVATION

Award for Best Female Lead in a Musical. Sara co-created and composed with Anais West the slam poetry musical titled *Poly Queer Love Ballad*, which toured to Toronto, Edmonton, and Vancouver.

Poly Queer Love Ballad is a bold, intimate musical merging slam poetry with pop-folk music. Nina, a polyamorous bisexual poet, meets Gabbie, a monogamous lesbian songwriter, at Cafe Deux Soleils. With two microphones, a loop pedal, and an array of instruments, they struggle to reconcile their fierce mutual attraction with their opposing perspectives on love. The show explores polyamory and queerness, aiming to create a new representation of intimacy that isn't confined by genre, medium, or societal obligations.

Nina is a polyamorous bisexual woman in her twenties, eager, bookish, and always trying to do the right thing. An undergrad lit student by day, an aspiring slam poet by night, Nina is already involved with a bisexual man when she starts dating Gabbie. Throughout the play, she wrestles with her romantic commitment to the monogamous Gabbie and how it challenges her ethics of autonomy and personal freedom. In the monologue, Nina's male partner describes his first date with another man, leading her to experience compersion for the first time.

Poly Queer Love Ballad was first produced by the frank theatre company, Zee Zee Theatre, and the Queer Arts Festival, Vancouver, on March 5, 2019. It was performed by Anais West and Sara Vickruck, directed by Julie McIsaac, with dramaturgy by Joanna Garfinkel, production design by Jessica Han, costume and set design by Alaia Hamer, lighting design by Harika Xu, stage management by Sammie Hatch, and production by Anais West and Sara Vickruck.

✦✦✦

NINA: My other lover sits beside me.
He's the serious type, shirt buttoned up tight
but tonight
he's boyish and flustered.

He slept with a guy.
His first.

He describes their date.
Feeds me morsels of their late night
beach side tryst:
A drunken kiss
after fervent texts,
timid touching comes next.

We're giddy,
beer moving past our lips,
my thigh against his,
our negative space electric.

Is this compersion?
The opposite of jealousy?

Jealousy broke me, once.
As a kid, I didn't wear my difference well.
I was pushed to the peripheries.
Unwanted and alone,
I fed on my envy,
I ate nothing else.

In the doctor's office,
belly bulging with water
to push the scale past ninety pounds,
I heard the threat of hospitalization
and ended my hunger strike.

Tonight,
I'm full with someone else's joy.

With him,
difference is our commonality.
When we touch, we transfer our exile heat.
When we kiss, stories thrum between our lips,
our bodies like books, opening.

A DRUNK LESBIAN LOVE AFFAIR

THALÍA GONZÁLEZ KANE

Thalía González Kane (she/her) is an award-winning queer, Ecuadorian Canadian multidisciplinary artist. She has worked as a performer, voice-over artist, playwright, director, designer, composer, choreographer, and producer in Canada, England, Ireland, Scotland, Sweden, Czechia, and various states in the USA. Thalía is a co-founder of Got Your Back Canada, co-chair of outACTRAto, and the artistic director of Crave Productions. She has been published by University of Toronto Press, *Intermission Magazine*, and *Canadian Theatre Review*, where she is also an editor. Thalía was named a playwright to watch by Playbill in 2020 for her show *A Drunk Lesbian Love Affair*. The play was also a finalist for the Oscar Wilde Prize for Best New Writing in Dublin, Ireland.

"The fact is that I love you. I am drunk. And I love you." They're young. They're drunk. They're in love . . . until they sober up. *A Drunk Lesbian Love Affair* chronicles the escapades of Sally and her "drunk lesbian lover" through a haze of whiskey and wine. This one-person show explores the vulnerability of love, our relationships to sexuality, queerness, and coming into one's own. A tender-hearted comedy, *A Drunk Lesbian Love Affair* combines millennial discourse, poeticism, and movement in the search for a sober love.

Sally is a queer cis-woman in her mid-twenties. She hasn't quite figured out what she wants from life yet, but she lives it boldly anyway. She bounces between jobs and has the spirit of an artist. She is an old soul and an absolute romantic—but she tries not to let it show. Note that her attempts are rarely successful. She has a heart of gold and the best of intentions, but in the end, is only human.

A Drunk Lesbian Love Affair was first produced at the International Dublin Gay Theatre Festival, Dublin, Ireland, on May 6, 2019. It was performed by Thalía González Kane, directed by Eimear Keating, with stage management and design by Lisa Barry.

✦✦✦

The morning after. SALLY *is a mess. She is not home.*

SALLY: Fuck.

I didn't go home.
We stumbled home.
We watched *Friends* on Netflix for five minutes then wanted to go to sleep because we were both drunk at midnight in the middle of the week.

We kissed.
Bliss.
I brought my body closer to hers.
I put my arm under her head so I could caress her back.
My other hand on her waist.
It was so slow.
So still.
And then—
Pulses.

The pulse of your heart.
The pulse of my veins.
The pulse of my body touching your body and that pulse growing into one.
You lean in, and our lips meet.
You kiss me. I kiss you back hard.
I lose my breath.

Literally.
I cough for half a second then I get it together because suddenly all I know how to do is kiss you.

It's the only language I understand because right now, nothing could be more important than kissing your lips.
Tasting the stale beer on your breath.
But in my mind, your mouth is a wonderland I want to get lost in for the night.

And that, I do.

Moans and gasps fill the space until we find a moment of pause, rest.

Bliss.

I don't know if it's ever been like this.

This . . . it's incredible.
Right now it is you and I and I—
I don't have any hang ups or hookups or whatever the fuck else excuses I make.
Because right now
I love you.

(Did she just say that?)

Despite what everyone else thinks.
Despite what you think.
Hell, despite what I think.

The fact is that I love you.

I am drunk.

And I love you.

And in morning, when I am sober, I won't.

I can't.

So right now, I am going to stay drunk and in love with you as long as I possibly can.

> SALLY *recalls the night and feels it through her body. She repeats every movement and every moment until it is engrained in her body so she won't forget.*
>
> *She doesn't want to forget.*
>
> *Can't forget.*

A GODAWFUL SMALL AFFAIR

HAYLEY ST. JAMES

Hayley St. James (they/them), based in New York and Boston, is a Boston-born early-career playwright, lyricist-in-training, dramaturge, and occasional performer and assistant director. A non-binary pansexual on the autism spectrum, they are deeply passionate about seeing themselves and their communities represented truthfully in all media, theatre first and foremost. In their theatrical work, they strive to marry authentic representation with hypertheatrical, surreal, meta, and intimate twists; they also have a thing for imaginary friends, ghosts, aliens, and well-handled pop culture references. Their plays include *For Leonora, Or, Companions*, a play with puppetry elements about life and love on the autism and 2SLBGTQ+ spectrum; *Shrike and Magpie*, a ten-minute jewel heist comedy with a dash of lesbian intrigue; and their Affair Trilogy, consisting of *A Godawful Small Affair* and the one-act play *It's Confusing, These Days*.

A lesbian couple are put in an unexpected U-haul situation and a touch-starved, non-binary stoner is visited by the alien angel ghost of David Bowie. A pandemic rages outside. A wall separates them, but they're all about to be connected, sort of. Can a relationship become routine if there's nothing else? Can life? And can a change in routine become a blessing? This messy, kind of sad, kind of hopeful, and deeply intimate play explores touch, longing, time, and routine in the age of COVID-19, and what this pandemic has done to us. And also David Bowie.

Luca is a twenty-something, non-binary bisexual with short, faded green-dyed hair. They're an ambivert, with an addictive personality, and probably somewhere on the autism spectrum, who hyperfixates easily; also a stoner and David Bowie fan. In this monologue, Luca has recently had a surprising intimate moment with their next-door neighbour Jodie, and has had a very vivid dream because of it.

✦✦✦

LUCA is sitting on the edge of their bed, facing the general direction of the rightmost wall. They are in just their briefs; their binder is on the floor. They look on edge.

LUCA: I just had the . . . craziest fucking dream.
I was in a forest, on a mysterious planet.
The trees were made of dark green crystal and the grass was made of finely-spun yellow glass.
The sky looked like a kaleidoscope, just like I've been told.
The trees were populated by small flocks of pink birds, with huge shiny black eyes and funky golden beaks and long fluffy tails and luxurious feathery wings.
I was in the forest with my ex.
We were running through this forest, holding hands, in flowing translucent white robes.
Well, actually, they were running ahead, pulling me by the hand.
We ran and ran and ran until we came to this huge wall in the middle of the forest that stretched for what looked like miles in either direction.
And when we got to the wall, my ex pushed me against the wall and started kissing me.
We were kissing, and kissing, and kissing.
Like we hadn't kissed in months or years and were filling ourselves with kisses to make up for lost time.
And then they took off my robe, and I took off theirs.
And we just sat there, naked, and held each other.
We just sat backs against this massive wall in the middle of a crystal forest on a planet in a faraway kaleidoscope galaxy, and held each other.
And then the strangest thing happened.
The sky ripped open and golden light poured from a crack in the swirling purple ether.
The light tore into the wall . . . and through my ex.

As the wall fell, they disintegrated in my hands into a pile of softly glowing diamonds.

And then the pile of diamonds floated to the other side of the wall, and turned into green crystal leaves . . . and the green crystal leaves turned into . . . well . . . a breathing, alive, flesh-and-blood, naked Jodie.

Or what I imagine a naked Jodie to look like.

I'm not proud of that, but . . . it's a dream.

Anyway.

Dream Jodie stared at my nakedness. I stared at hers.

We didn't exchange any words.

I just walked through the break in the wall, and held her. And she held me. We just held each other, for a long, long time. We kissed a bit, but mostly just held each other.

We just . . . took comfort in contact. In touch.

It was nice. It was warm. She was warm.

The sky above pulsated and twinkled.

And then I woke up, sweating, with wetness all over my hands.

Must have been touching myself before I went to sleep high again.

When I woke up, I checked to see what I was listening to before I passed out. I was listening to "Heroes." And I thought about my dream, and I thought about the time Jodie came over.

She's just . . . on the other side of the wall. It's like "Heroes," . . . but instead of the Berlin Wall it's our shitty apartment building.

OUTSTRETCHED

EMILY POWERS

Emily Powers (she/her/hers) is a playwright/comedian from Toronto. She studied at the Upright Citizens Brigade, the Second City Conservatory, and the Groundlings. Her plays have been mounted internationally. She's won the Robertson Davies Playwriting Award twice and was a finalist in SheNYC Festival and Scranton Scratch Night hosted by *Saturday Night Live*'s Heidi Gardner. You know Emily as the girl with unrequited yearning on your recreational soccer team.

Four years after the death of his sister, Diana, Hyatt finds a collection of video clips she intended to make into a short film, many centering around Kate, Diana's first love. Hyatt gets in contact with Kate and has to come to terms with his sister's queerness in an act of closure. Lines between the characters get blurry and merge as they learn how to (or forget how to) navigate youth, loss, and memory.

The timeline of the play is falling in on itself and the language itself is corroding. The monologue is performed like a slam poem as Kate is recalling the earlier stages of her relationship with Diana and the queer community she came up in.

Outstretched was first produced by Trinity College Dramatic Society as a part of the U of T Drama Festival, 2019, at Hart House, Toronto, on February 8, 2019. It was performed by Victoria Watson Sepejak, Hannah Fleisch, and Ezera Beyene; directed by Jennifer Dufton; produced by Ishani Ranjan and Annie MacKillican; and designed by Alberta Saunders, Mads Ceilidh, Sanna Wani, Emily Johnstone, Rebecca Chess, and Tuhi Sen.

✦ AN OPEN LETTER TO THE GAY BOYS WHO GRAB MY BOOBS WHEN THEY ARE DRUNK ✦

KATE GLENDALE: If I wanted a spiky-haired jock to honk my tits like they're clown noses, I'd go to more frat parties.
Did you catch that? The fear behind my meanness.
I spread snark over whimper in thick layers
like a molasses armour
because somewhere down the road I was told I shouldn't say no to you.

You—
legs spread out on the subway
three seats for your gangly knees
popping, cracking
automaton boy—
You—
heavy stride, head up
straight course down the street,
I move for you.

I am not a space to be filled.
Which is to say, I am mine before I'm anybody else's.

But I move anyway.
Which is to say—I'm scared of you.
You—
You are my friend.
I haven't had a guy touch me like that in a very long time.
But you know this, because you call me dyke almost every day
like my name is too many syllables for your mouth
you chew and lick—
lips too full—
funny,
that the only time you've had your mouth on a vagina
is with the word cunt on your tongue as you greet me.
You—
and the gay men who take the words of black women
and stuff them into their mouths
—their pockets—
commodify culture
because what's a woman if it can't be mocked.
and what are words when they are not funnier said by a man.

The white gay men who forget Stonewall wasn't their victory to have.

You think you understand womanhood because you like men
but sexuality is not a free pass to my body.
Your gayness does not excuse your maleness,
just as my queerness does not negate my whiteness.
And your unwanted touch is not a joke.

The first time I touched someone's breasts,
I was so nervous I asked her permission three times.
Shaky—younger than noon, flaxen hair—
soft on my unbalmed lips.
but your touch weighs heavier than mine and
I worry she won't remember my softness beneath it.

I want her to see her breasts as something that are fully hers.
Which is to say, she is hers before she is mine.
Which is to say, I love her.
Have you ever loved someone like that?

If I asked you to stop,
You would say you weren't hurting me.
Like you aren't attracted to me yet my body still belongs to you—
You said I was too in my own head about, too full of myself.
I don't want to be full of anything *but* myself.

My freshman year
my straight roommate told me he thought
going down on a girl was gross.
I told him I liked giving her pleasure
and he just looked at me,
confused
wondering why I would kiss something
I was supposed to fuck.

CONCORD FLORAL

JORDAN TANNAHILL

Jordan Tannahill (he/him) is a playwright and two-time winner of the Governor General's Award for Drama. His plays have been translated into twelve languages and frequently explore the nature of belief, queer identity, power relations, and the body as a political subject.

Concord Floral is a million-square-foot abandoned greenhouse and a hangout for neighbourhood kids. But something has happened there. Something that nobody can talk about. And when two friends stumble upon the terrible secret buried there, they set off a chain of events that can't be stopped. *Concord Floral* reimagines Giovanni Boccaccio's medieval allegory *The Decameron* in a contemporary Toronto suburb, in which ten teens must flee a mysterious plague they have brought upon themselves.

Just Joey shares with the audience an encounter he had with the father of a classmate.

Concord Floral was written by Jordan Tannahill and developed over a three-year process with Erin Brubacher, Cara Spooner, and a group of teenagers from across the Greater Toronto Area. It was first produced by Suburban Beast and presented by at the Theatre Centre, Toronto, on October 12, 2014. It was performed by Liam Sullivan, Troy Sarju, Theo Gallaro, Melisa Sofi, Jessica Munk, Erum Khan, Sahra Del, Eartha Masek-Kelly, Rashida Shaw, and Jovana Miladinovic; directed by Erin Brubacher, Cara Spooner, and Jordan Tannahill; with composition and sound design by Christopher Willes; lighting design by Kimberly Purtell; stage management by Laura Hendrickson; and dramaturgy by Erin Brubacher.

✦✦✦

JUST JOEY: I'm learning to get better
At a lot of things
Knowing more about the world
Capitals and countries
How to dress
How to take better selfies
I post a selfie and it gets forty likes in ten minutes
Monday at four o'clock: that's prime time for likes
Then I take a few cock pics and post them on Grindr
Nineteen-year-old, 7-inch, brown hair, hazel eyes
Looking to hook up nearby, can't host, healthy
Looking for 18–30 but open to older if you're hot
No chubs, not too hairy
No creepers or pic collectors
Serious for 2nite
Will bottom for the right guy
I get twenty-four replies in the first hour
Mostly weirdos
A few guys living downtown
Students
Potheads
A twinky skater
Can't tell if he's real
The second I tell them I'm living in Vaughan they're like, "Forget it"
Or just don't reply
I'm like—it's just an hour on the TTC
I'd ride an hour for a blow job, wouldn't you?
Maybe they get lots
Maybe it's just like a bowl of cereal if you live downtown
And then around midnight I start a back-and-forth with a guy from Vaughan
"Are you really nineteen?"

"Ya, you?"
"Thirty-five"
"You wanna get sucked off?
"Do you bottom?"
"Maybe"
"Have you bottomed before?"
"Not really"
"Lol, you don't know?"
"I can't host"
"Neither can I"
"I can give you head in your car. Or a park?"
"What about Concord Floral? You know it?"
"The greenhouse?"
"Meet you there in an hour?"
I'm like "Um, okay, but bring condoms," and he's like "Lol 'k 'k"
He isn't thirty-five
He's probably forty-five
Maybe fifty
I know him
He's the dad of a kid in my school, a grade younger
I've seen him shovelling his driveway in his suit some mornings
He has grey on his temples
In the dark of the greenhouse his cock is in shadows
but I can tell it's huge, veiny
I imagine him fucking his wife with it
I don't know if I should ask him to put a condom on
I don't want him to think I don't know what I'm doing
and maybe I'm not doing it right,
am I supposed to be blowing or is it just sucking
why isn't it called a suck job, and how should I be:
crouched down or squatting or kneeling?
It hurts to kneel on the broken glass—
and then all of a sudden he comes
He just grunts and I feel it in my mouth

and I stand up and spit it out
and like I'm still totally dressed
and as he's zipping his fly I notice these two eyes
glinting by the door of the greenhouse
A fox
I think it was watching us
The guy turns around and the fox darts into the field
"Hope he doesn't tell anyone," he chuckles
. . .
When I get home I have a shower
And then jerk off twice before heading to bed
Sometimes I feel insatiable
It's difficult to explain
I saw him a week or so later raking leaves
I was waiting for the bus
He looked right at me but didn't recognize me
Or if he did, he didn't let on

SHAME

MACKENZIE MCCALLUM-MALLORY

Mackenzie Mccallum-Mallory (he/him) is a transgender live performance artist, playwright, and image maker in Toronto, Ontario. Selected credits include the Eyes on Beginnings series (Toronto Dance Theatre, 2023), Summer Apprenticeship (Clay and Paper Theatre, 2023), Night of Dread 2023 (Clay and Paper Theatre), Queer Youth Cabaret (Soulpepper, 2022), QueerCab: Playing With Abundance (Buddies in Bad Times Theatre, 2022), *MASK4MASK* (Living Labs, Theatre@York, 2021–22), *Skinny Dipping Lake* (Audio Theatrica Vol. 1), *Fruiting Bodies* (playGround Festival, 2022), and *SHAME* (Past Lives Production Company 5290 Festival). He is continuing to develop his solo show, *BODY PLAN*, and a projection-based adaptation of *Giselle*. Mac is also a recent graduate of York University's B.F.A. in Performance Creation with a focus on playwrighting and devised theatre.

Set against the backdrop of Toronto's gay club scene, *SHAME* follows Tom and Dan, two queer men exploring their sexualities for the first time while navigating their relationships to gender, consent, and their own bodies. Moving to a small town in Southern Ontario, Tom and Dan must contend with their own messes of masculinity and navigate feelings of shame surrounding their desires as they are sucked into the gay club scene. Mixing dialogue and poetry, *SHAME* explores the joys and pitfalls of being a young queer man contending with sex, hookups, gender crises, sexual responsibility, and a dainty piece of red lingerie. This play has a content warning for sexual assault.

Tom has recently moved in with Dan, his former roommate and long-time childhood friend, after a year apart. Tom realizes his burgeoning queerness as he gains freedom and anonymity, moving to Toronto from Lucan, Ontario, though it's still something he struggles to express and wants to keep hidden. Things have also changed between Tom and Dan in the year since they were apart, as feelings have grown on both sides—without the other knowing. As a celebration of their reunion, and in an attempt to show Tom "the big city," Dan drags Tom to a local night club where he is able to express himself fully and see himself represented for the first time.

SHAME was first produced as a virtual show by Past Lives Production Company, Toronto, on August 5, 2020. It was performed by Felix Hao, Anthony Palermo, Evan Kuhn, and Rashawn Thakoordeen; directed by Mackenzie Mccallum-Mallory and Sarah Miller; with dramaturgy by Sarah Miller; sound design by Hannah Rocca; media design by David Browne; costume design by Billie Wilner; music composition by David Browne; and video editing by Varnika Grover and Mackenzie Mccallum-Mallory.

✦ THE CLUB ✦

Outside the club. Bass booming. Shifts take us from one moment to the next—each moment takes us deeper into the night.

TOM: How much? Twenty. For two? Ten each. Great, thanks. Stamp? Shit, it's packed. This place is great. You'll love it. If you say so . . . What's up? Just busy, is all. Busy is good. Busy is *annoying*. C'mon. I promised us drinks. You're eager. I've never seen you like this. Looking for someone?

Shift. In the bathroom.

The bathroom is like being in the bottom of a ship.
Hollow echo.
Tile floor.
Metal door.
Closing at 25 per cent speed.
The bass of the club a heartbeat—
A fist against the door.

There's two men in the bathroom.
Maybe they met at the bar.
I hear them in the stall as I stand at the urinal.
Clanging against the metal, lock jingling.
Sloppy.
Tongue on tongue or tongue on—
Who knows.

God.
Shouldn't even matter cuz I have to piss but pissing with your neck craning over your shoulder will get an orthopedic surgeon or a physiotherapist in your bed faster than you can say fibrodysplasia ossificans progressiva.

Sorry.
That's the stone man syndrome,
the one where your body turns to bone.

Like now.
Craned.
Looking through the gap between the lock and the door
trying to glimpse a little piece of flesh . . .

A moan. The bathroom door opens. The club returns. Shift. On the dance floor. TOM *is a bad dancer.*

In my body
Really *in* my body.
And then out of it again,
lost in the bodies, the noise, the movement
bump and grind and bash and stomp and trip
I can feel the bass moving through me.
Each individual waveform oscillating in
my cells
my blood
my skin
my nipples
my cock
my balls
my heart.

And suddenly a feeling of arousal, a feeling of elation, yelling and screaming and whooping and hollering and drinking more and getting more drunk and more drunk and after a while, after a while shots get easy—'specially when someone else is buying—and then spilling out, colours spilling out and melting and revealing the street and the coolness of the sweat on my forehead and your forehead and the way the ground feels and the expanse of the city and the people in it, the expanse of my heart opening, your heart opening, the way that our skin tingles and how we can't hear anything, our ears ringing and the huge and giant and LOUD city feels so quiet, and calm, and silent.

And then we go home.

It was great.

ROW

T. BERTO

T. Berto (they/them) has had plays presented in Ontario, BC, Alberta, the Yukon, and in New York State; including five short plays at Edmonton's Loud and Queer Festival. The winner of an Arch and Bruce Brown Foundation Award, their play *ROW* was presented, in various forms, at Buddies in Bad Times Theatre as part of *Free Jane*, at the Roundhouse Theatre in Vancouver as part of the Clean Sheets festival, and the 2014 SummerWorks Festival. They have won the Toronto Fringe Festival Best New Play prize twice; for their first play *BASH*, in 2000 and for their play *The Singularity of Being* in 2009. They are presently developing their new play *ANYOX*. They live in Guelph.

ROW is about Sonny, a man whose sexual objectification and body-commodification informs his persona. Yet Sonny dismisses the perks of being a wealthy man's plaything; he is attracted instead to the man's absolute power. What he seeks is a complex dynamic of total submission and, yet conversely, total control. The play visits Sonny in three timelines, which eventually converge at its climax. The first takes place in the moments of youth sexuality, where power relationships and institutional abuse are explored. The second timeframe shows Sonny much older, having left the sex trade, offering nuggets of caution he has learned from his trade. The third timeline shows Sonny in his thirties, in the "now" of the play.

Sonny knows nothing other than being a "kept" man. Now in his mid-thirties and freshly freed of his last long-term client, he has just arrived in a hurricane-ravaged city and is actively searching for his next keeper. The night begins as he encounters one of three men, each of whom he judges for their suitability as perhaps his next host. Out of practice, and aware his appeal in lessened by his advanced years in the trade, he cautiously explores, and tests the suitability of the men to whom he presents himself. He is briefly amused by the cachet he can still muster, but forces himself to stay on mission. After all, at this point in his life, there are few, if any, options open to him.

ROW was first produced by Theatre Passe Muraille at the SummerWorks Theatre Festival, Toronto, on August 9, 2014. It was performed by Dillan Chiblow, Garret C. Smith, and Billy Merasty; with cello performance and music composition by Cris Derksen; stage management and lighting design by Brittany Ryan; production design by Isidra Cruz; production assistance by Jenny So; and photography featuring Dillan Chiblow by Max Telzerow.

✦ SONNY ✦

SONNY is a serial "kept boy"; fit but jaded, in his thirties, recently emancipated. As he's aged, he's had to find progressively less "ideal," but more particular keepers. He enters a bar.

SONNY: It's hard to tell if the corrugated metal around the walls is part of its actual building, or just meant to hint at what's within. It is hurricane-town after all, and there's a whole bunch of buildings barely held together with chicken wire and chipboard. Sometimes only a resurrected, plaster Madonna perched on the rubble lets you know that anyone's caring for anything. So the black tin panels that cover the joint's exterior aren't out of place. But still, when you take it all in, you kind of expect a lame rottweiler, or an abandoned Oldsmobile, to be parked out front. There isn't but, well, some things are in transition.

The second I'm inside though, it's familiar. Mmm. I can't remember the last time I smelled smoke in a bar—I've been kept, for years, up in prissy-town after all—so when that perfumed glove of tobacco grabs my face at the door, it kinda takes me back.

And as I step in, I can tell there's other things here, familiar. Things that I miss.

It's pitch-black at first. But you can navigate other ways: the smell of leather, men's bodies; a pissy stink at the side, by the head, cummy in the darker corners and by the stairs at the back, and dank and sugary where the rode-hard, twenty-something barboy spills over-sized shots at the bar. And there's the murmurs too. They whip past, like pucks across the backboards, when they see me.

"Tourist."
"Slummer."
"In over his head."

But I'm used to it. Or was. I always seem to be able to find this sort of place all over, wherever. And it's always the same reaction. Should expect it.

After all, I'm clean and kinda twinked in a tank and all, and the light is kind. Just bought the shirt and the shorts, left the rest in a trash can seventy miles upstream. There's not a hint of where I might've just drifted in from. But I know what I'm doing. *(gesturing to his body)* It isn't about the packaging anyways, now is it?

But I'm a bit rusty. Been a while.

So. I get two beer in me real fast, backed with a JD. I can order my own. As much as I like, now. And I've got blood pulsing to every part of me. I need to hold steady. Not that I need courage. Hell no. Just a little . . . stability, a little oil on the water. Ready myself.

Some Daddy likes me at the bar already. I was targeting the back stairs, but I can stay here awhile. He's probably only eight or ten years older, but he's weather-beaten, real crusty, stained with nicotine and a thousand nights on that stool.

He lets his hand sneak up the leg of my baggy shorts, treasure hunting. I can play this for a bit, and who knows? Never judge a book . . . but I'm not promising anything.

So, I bum a smoke, and inhale the forbiddenness. Can't do this up north.

Aaah.

Between his fingers on my ass and the Marlboro in my lungs, it spins me good. And the dated fag-pop thumping in my ears is the perfect finish. *(exhales big)* Right. I'm here.

Daddy looks to explore up a little further. A little rougher. So, okay. Let's see how this plays. His palm is like greasy sandpaper up the inside of my thigh . . . pushing . . . testing. And then he *offers* me a drink.

Hmmm. He should've just ordered me one. A bad sign. He's having some syrupy thing. Old boozer's delight. So, I test him. I tell him it's tequila or not. He looks away, a bit pissed at the gall.

There's a minute, and then he dangles a twenty for the bar boy, who snaps to him like a cadet. He orders his rum thingy. The boy conjures it by rote: napkin, coaster, ice, booze, mix, fruit, straw, boom!—right between Daddy's elbows on the bar.

But before the boy touches the bill, Daddy finishes with:

(a New Orlean's drawl) "And a Cuervo for our lost sailor here."

—without so much as even a twitch my way.
Barboy looks at me, asking with his eyes for a second if I know what I'm doing, and then:
"Lemon and salt?" . . . like it's a palliative.
"No. Tobasco would please me better." Giving back a touch of drawl, for his pleasure.
Daddy's head twitches now. Barboy lets go a tiny smirk.

He pours, and then starts shaking in the hot stuff, looking at me out of the corner of his eye, like I'm supposed to tell him "when." I pretend I don't see.

He brings it in a minute, likely blood red now, its vinegar cutting through the wafts. Daddy taps it with his.

(a New Orlean's drawl) "Up your ass."

He drinks deeply.

"Or somebody's," I counter.

Pound.
Swallow.
Beer.
Exhale . . . There's a point about eight seconds after tequila that a little shiver runs through.
Aaahhh.
I lean against the bar for that. Hold my breath. It's good. Visceral.

He's exploring further now. His hand is about to score but then . . . but then he gets just a tiny bit . . . tentative. Uh-oh. *That's* no good. And now, he almost completely stops. He's done in my book. So I've got to shut him down. I drop something and bend to pick it up, forcing his hand to behave. He gets the cue. Now he's wondering about his next move, just sitting here, cool but tamed, unsure . . .

So I do a really slow scope about the room, pretending I'm not aware of him at all. I can see leaving him after a spell . . . that'll make me some trophy value in the room. And it's working already. Eyes are on me.

So. One more beer, and then the back stairs. Now *I* hold out a bill, but I'm low on Barboy's list. Daddy sees it and is gonna move, thinking he can get back some chance, but I touch his leathery shoulder, saying:

"No, definitely my pleasure."
(drawl) "Suit yourself."
And he sees me eyeing the back stairs while waiting.
(drawl) "You know what's up there, do you?"
"I'm gathering a pretty good idea."

"Like *you're* an authority on it, Carson"—some wizened old queen next to him pipes in.

Barboy, suddenly there, adds:
"Yeah, when did *you* last climb up?"

And then to me . . . "Another?" . . . pointing at my bottle.
Mmm.

(drawl) "I don't feel the particular need, to find pleasures elsewise of where I am."
There's a bit of laughter all around. He's done with this. A little pissed.

(drawl) "Off you go then, soldier."
"I thought I was '*sailor*'"
(drawl) "You be something . . . after you go up there. We'll see."
"My thanks again . . . " but he throws his hand my way, *(extending a long arm out, palm first)* already cast his judgment, done, not hearing.

And I'm off. On my mission. But I can feel his eyes lingering, wanting, with every slow step, I climb up the stairs.
And that's a good thing.

GOOD GIRL

NORA VISION

Nora Vision (she/they) is a playwright, drag queen, and robotic emissary sent from the future to save humanity. "Born and raised" in Winnipeg, Nora has produced and performed in the Winnipeg Fringe Festival, Toronto SketchFest, and Ladyfest in their current hometown of Montréal. A recent graduate from National Theatre School's Playwriting Program, Nora's play *Sycophant* was produced as part of the school's New Words Festival, May 2023. They are a recent participant of the Banff Playwrights Lab, and hosted and produced the Big & Fruity Open Mic and SEANCE: A Cabaret of Queer Performance. As an artificially intelligent robot, Nora is interested in creating work that confronts identity, culture, and propaganda, questioning how each contributes, limits, and undermines one's sense of reality. A performance artist at heart, Nora's theatrical writings place her own identity at the forefront to challenge assumptions of subjectivity and viewership.

As twenty-first century fascism takes shape, the internet becomes a place for not just self-discovery, but projection. Viz, an isolated, lonely twenty-something non-binary queer spends more time online in the midst of a global lockdown, and discovers pieces of themself they never knew. Connecting with other self-identified sissies, Viz experiments with sissy hypno—a porn genre that promises the behavioural modification of curious young boys into feminine submissive ones. Turned on and excited by the pieces of themself they never knew, Viz falls deeper into the game, eventually committing to the service of a faceless, voiceless, identity-less figure hidden behind the screen. As Viz feels more and more comfortable with their own desire to submit, they must reckon with their increasingly growing fear that something is terribly, terribly wrong.

Viz has never felt comfortable expressing their own needs, preferring instead to fulfill the needs of those around them. After breaking up with their long-term partner, they are left not knowing what they really want. In this moment, Viz has begun serving the anonymous person they met online and is being instructed how to speak while masturbating. Although they have done this a few times now, this prayer begins to transform as they diverge from the script and become caught up in their own pleasure.

✦✦✦

They masturbate.

VIZ: I am a good girl.

I like myself. I like the way I am, and the way I look.

I am not scared of judgment.

I am confident, charming, kind, and forward-thinking.

I make others happy.

I am an angel. I see the world in unique and beautiful ways.

I love myself. I love my body.

I love to train my mind and body.

I feel clear. Real. Tangible.

I submit to myself. The trans futurist Goddess of creation and orgasmic reckoning.

My body is a vessel of pleasure in service to the universal consciousness.

When I cum, the world trembles.

Neptune can feel the aching of my emptiness.

Aliens, in dimensions beyond conception, see my open mouth and throb, erect in ways never before known.

The Earth is my sex toy.

I am its slut—its submissive piece of flesh and wanting.

Shooting, leaking ejaculate that carries within the secrets to humanity.

The Future is Stored in the Balls.

Quaking, quantum possibility.

Alternate realities shift into focus, rapidly changing between the Is and the Isn't. My sexuality the herald of regeneration.

Trumpets blare as I bring forward the new world. Birthed of my cock.

The world is in my head.

I submit to the TransDivinity.

Godforce and nothing else.

They work through me.

Reckoning cums only in violence.

But peace cums only through reckoning.

Pain

Submissions

Obedience

Glory

I leak the World.

The universe slowly escapes from my *(cunt)*

I am a Good Girl.

LIKE ORPHEUS

BRETT DAHL

Brett Dahl (they/them) is a queer director, writer, actor, drag performer, and educator based in Amiskwacîwâskahikan (Edmonton), Sikóóhkotok (Lethbridge), and Mohkinstsis (Calgary). Brett's first play, *Like Orpheus*, premiered at Theatre Outré and continued to tour to the International Dublin Gay Theatre Festival in Ireland, and OUTstages with Intrepid Theatre. In 2020, *Pretty Ugly* was produced by the Alberta Queer Calendar Project and Cardiac Theatre. Brett has been part of the Major Matt Mason Collective Wildfire Development Unit, Alberta Playwrights' Network RBC Emerging Artist program, and is currently in the Bad Hat Theatre's New Bad Ideas program. Brett was the recipient of Theatre Calgary's Stephen Hair Emerging Actor Award in 2015, the Lieutenant Governor of Alberta Emerging Artist Award in 2018, and the Cultural Leader RBC Emerging Artist Award in Calgary in 2020. Brett is currently writing a queer TYA musical called *Bee Beeautiful*. Brett is a graduate of the B.F.A. acting and M.F.A. directing programs at the University of Alberta, and is the new artistic director of Theatre Outré in Lethbridge.

Like Orpheus is a candid dive into queer club culture and the trauma of sexual assault. Told through poetic text, visceral movement, and an evocative soundscape, *Like Orpheus* is an episodic drama moving through a cacophony of thoughts and dreams. The play is divided into three parts: the Boy dancing in an underground club, which results in a violent assault; years later, the Boy (now the Man) is haunted by recurring dreams and haunted by a vision of his younger self; and finally the Man's and Boy's worlds collide as the lines of dreaming and reality are blurred, asking the Man to turn around to face his past. *Like Orpheus* is an exploration of what love, trauma, and fear do to us from the inside out.

The Boy: in his early twenties. More Berlin-fuck-boi than innocent youth—sexy, broody, and ethereal. No stranger to the nightlife, the Boy "returning to the club . . . a dark, dark place that feels like home" has been partying all night and is lost in ecstatic escape of dancing and "snow and speed and smoke and sweat." After finding a mysterious stranger on the dance floor, the Boy is drugged and raped in the back alley behind the club. The monologue begins as the Boy, still in a state of paralysis, leaves the club to drive home and fragments of the assault replay in his mind.

Like Orpheus was first produced by Theatre Outré in Lethbridge, Alberta, on February 25, 2019. It was performed by Brett Dahl and Kevin Jesuino; directed by Jay Whitehead; with dramaturgy by Damien Atkins; stage management and assistant direction by Jordan Payne; choreography by Brett Dahl, Kevin Jesuino, and Jay Whitehead; sound design by Lyndsay Labrecque; costume and set design by Deonie Hudson; and lighting design by Dave Smith. *Like Orpheus* was adapted into a short film in 2021 with the support of the Canada Council for the Arts Digital Now initiative and Theatre Outré. It was performed by Brett Dahl and David Ley and directed by Jay Whitehead, with assistant direction by Andrés Moreno, choreography by Kevin Jesuino, sound design by Lyndsay Labrecque, production management by Danielle Smith, director of photography by Blake Everden, and dramaturgy and editing by Leigh Rivenbark.

✦✦✦

Alone, the Boy shivers, unable to speak at first.

His body lets out small tremors. He struggles to comprehend what happened. Disoriented, coming out of shock, his thoughts are cacophonous and haunting. Through the monologue, he "drives" home but he stands still—trapped in a paralysis.

BOY: riding home
quiet

through the city streets
blurring
lights
wet
roads
damp air
cold feet.

its chases me
i held it off
but it's late
and i'm high
and it
comes
unexpected—first in small waves—hitting the back of my body—then crashing—
collapsing on my heart—holding my lungs—viced in an unbearable grip
a haunting i can't escape.

ican'tescape

i must be dreaming
dreaming while waking
something keeps
holding me off
beckoning

my eyes . . .
were no longer my eyes . . .
my hands were no longer my hands . . .
my body buzzes
images
seared into memory—
imprints
demonic
red
everything was red.
everythingwasred

his hands.
beast like.
gripping me like thunder.
i can smell him on me.
me on me.
his cock.
my blood.
i smell him

and he enters my body
and i am cold
and i am empty
and i—

feel of the *weight* of his body on mine—of being lost and weightless—*his* body moving in the shape of an animal

in an out

like a fire—ignited—wild and untamed—and the unshakeable feeling of being invaded—eaten alive from the inside—a terrible chaos grows inside me . . .

the air is thick and

i still see his face.

see his face. see his face see his face see his face his face his face
hisfacehisfacehisface

THE LAWN (SEVERE ABBREVIATIONS)

LOGAN WILLIAMS

Logan Williams (he/him) is a queer performance-maker, writer, producer, and scholar working in visual culture, theatre, and curatorial studies. He aims to relocate the drama of the theatre to alternative spaces through explorations in embodiment and intimacy. Williams combines affect theory, queer ethics, and performance studies through curatorial projects and theatrical interventions that grapple with contemporary conceptions of home.

The man grows up on a lawn made of hyperartificial Astroturf. Surrounded by glossy items like a weed whacker, a barbeque, and a sprinkler, he tends to the lawn as a means of survival; to keep hidden his true desires. It is not until he meets the projection of the young man that he begins to grapple with his carnal desires. In a turbulent climax, the projection of the young man rapes the man, forcing the man to confront the violent constructs of the lawn and the objects used to maintain it, asking how do we forgive our oppressors in a cancel culture climate? Moreover, what hegemonic structures perpetuate the fears of our own pleasures? And can anything be pleasurable under the glistening auspices of capitalism?

The man wears a slip, covered in blood, semen, water, sweat, cigarette smoke, and charcoal. He is anywhere from eighteen to thirty. The projection of the young man is just that: a projection. He is beautiful.

the lawn (Severe Abbreviations) was developed with the support of the Canada Council for the Arts; the Playwrights Theatre Centre, Vancouver; and Title 66, Montréal.

✦✦✦

Note: the script is written in an unconventional style and leaves the interpretation to the producers whether the text is spoken aloud or not. For this submission, the following excerpt should be read aloud.

the man stumbles his way around the Astroturf

he leaves the curtain drawn across the back of the lawn with lazy half-heartedness

the bottles have collected dew from the sprinkler their labels peeling off in wet chunks
the man tripping over them
trying to pick them up

one after the other letting them fall thud

clearer against the curtain at the back of the lawn we see the projection of the young man staring at the man falling over his beer bottles catching a glimpse of the sizzling barbeque

wet from the sprinkler
the smell of charcoal all soaked in hose water

the man approaches the projection of the young man full of rage
and full of beer
winds up punches the projection of the young man the sounds of wet hands on a plastic curtain

the projection of the young man tosses the man to the ground with aggression

wobbling
woozy from the velocity and the alcohol the man is unable to get up

the projection of the young man looks around
unbuttons his pants
takes out his dick
grabs the man from behind and slaps his ass
the projection of the young man inserts his dick into the man violently
thrusting with anger and saliva

pouring down frothing
the man flails helpless
groaning and wailing and whimpering like a dog the sounds are painful
a baby left in the cold too frozen to scream

the boom box glitches and stops at varying intervals with every thrust a lag
with every whimper a skip in the sound

the projection of the young man comes

the projection of the young man carelessly lets the man flop to the ground
buttons up his pants
turns and walks into the distance

once the projection of the young man is far enough away he takes out his
dick again
and pisses

the projection of the young man vanishes

the man lies on the beer and water soaked Astroturf the sprinkler comes on
only there is no water
only the tick-tick-tick-tck-tck-tck-tck-tck

the stimulated stage moonlight
picks up shines on the bottles
making them twinkle
the flesh of the man all pallid and blue

many beats

the man reaches for the dejected silk slip he slides it on
lying on the Astroturf
in pain

it looks so uncomfortable
with great discipline the man rises

he pulls the rest of the curtains across the space the sprinkler comes on
the man does not reach for the soap like before instead standing lifeless

catatonic
he shivers slightly
the silk sticking to his wet body
clinging to his genitals
his nipples
only the sounds of water hitting the plastic

tick-tick-tick-tck-tck-tck-tck-tck

UNDERGROUND ABSOLUTE FICTION: A VIDEO ZINE

ANAIS WEST

Anais West (they/he) is a queer, trans writer, actor, and producer. They are also a Polish settler based on occupied xʷməθkʷəy̓əm (Musqueam), Sḵwx̱wú7mesh (Squamish), and səlilwətaʔɬ (Tsleil-Waututh) lands. Anais's work is interdisciplinary, merging theatre, film, music, and poetry to explore the multiplicity within gender, sexuality, culture, and self. Anais's writing includes *The Café* (ITSAZOO, Aphotic Theatre, and the PuSh Festival, Vancouver), the short theatrical film *Underground Absolute Fiction* (Rumble Theatre's Tremors Festival), the video-play hybrid *Kill Your Lovers* (Buddies in Bad Times Theatre's Rhubarb Festival, Tkarón:to, and the Fresh Fruit Festival, NYC), and the slam poetry musical *Poly Queer Love Ballad* (Queer Arts Festival, the frank theatre company, and Zee Zee Theatre, Vancouver, and Theatre Passe Muraille, Tkarón:to). Anais was awarded PTC's 2018 Fringe New Play Prize as well as first place in the 2023 Wildfire National Playwriting Competition. They've been nominated for two Jessie Richardson Awards, including Outstanding Original Script. As an actor, they've worked with Firehall Arts Centre, Savage Society, Théâtre La Seizième, Orange Noyée, the National Arts Centre, and more. Anais is the artistic producer at the frank theatre company.

Queers in communist Poland used self-published magazines to organize, get laid, and forge a sense of identity. In the wake of the arrest of Polish trans activist Margot Szutowicz, a Polish Canadian settler uses a fractured, theatre-film "zine" to seek answers. Through letters, social media posts, and a queer punk band's music videos, *Underground Absolute Fiction* complicates notions of "queer." The show reckons with the Western gaze on post-Soviet countries, asking whether queerness connects us across cultural rifts or if it's a site of imperialism.

Lena is a non-binary Polish Canadian settler in their late twenties. They are bold, imaginative, but deeply self-conscious. She's also an emerging filmmaker, looking to explore her cultural heritage through the medium of video. They ache deeply for community, connection, and belonging. Throughout the piece, Lena tries to connect with the Polish people in her life through a series of voice memos: first to her bisexual cousin, then her working-class grandfather, and lastly, an enigmatic Polish girl she meets at a café.

Underground Absolute Fiction: A Video Zine was first produced as part of Rumble Theatre's Tremors Festival, with associate production by the frank theatre company, Vancouver, on October 28, 2020. It was performed by Claire Love Wilson and Sara Vickruck, produced by Anais West, directed by Fay Nass, with videography by Christian Yves Jones, music direction by khattieQ, dramaturgy by Veronique West, cultural consultation by Julia Siedlanowska, music adaptation and transcription by Sara Vickruck, audio engineering by Eric Biskupski, and styling by Kimberly Ho.

✦✦✦

LENA: *Droga przyjaciółko,*

Dear friend,

Do you remember me?

Relax Cafe. Downtown Warsaw. It was summer. I was sitting under that red neon sign in my rainbow shorts, thighs scorching on a flimsy metal folding chair. I wasn't sure if it was the heat or my linguistic incompetence, but I was drenched in sweat. I was interviewing a straight man who photographed queers. When he left to refill his coffee, you turned in your chair and said:

"Are you looking for Polish queers?"

You couldn't help but eavesdrop. You told me you were an artist, that you were moving to Montréal next year. You asked me to go for a drink. Then you scrawled your Instagram on the back of my napkin.

When the man came back, I tried to return to my questions. But my eyes kept darting to the back of your head.

Do you remember the bar, Loko? We were the only ones in the basement, and the servers forgot about us, but somewhere between the white-brick walls, fake plants, and hideously patterned couch covers, you trusted me. A stranger. You said you'd probably never tell your family the truth. That they may already suspect it, but that naming it, presencing it in a room, would make it indisputable fact. So instead, you let the possibility hang between you over cabbage rolls, at your niece's first communion, in pointed remarks about your short hair.

You would never tell them. But it wasn't a tragedy. You chose your queer life, and your Polish life too. You could have both.

And in that moment, a possibility hung between us too.

Of you, fingering me in the back seat of your car.

Of you, teaching me how to say *kurwa* and *chuj.*

Of me, licking and sucking your clit till my mouth was sore.

Of you, telling your mom I'm your roommate, and her, calling me pretty in broken English.

Of you, teaching me to say *kocham cie.*

Of us, laughing as we call each other "friends," as we joke of being buried in the same grave, baffling your parents, invoking Maria Konopnicka.

Of us, unspoken, a trust so deep that naming it, presencing it in a room, would be unnecessary.

Do you remember that bar? That night?

Did you go to the protests? Are you safe? Are you still eavesdropping on girls in cafés?

ROOM 158

ÉRIC NOËL

TRANSLATED FROM FRENCH

BY RHIANNON COLLETT

Éric Noël (they/them) is a playwright, translator, and performer who graduated from Canada's National Theatre School French-language playwriting program. Based in Tiohtià:ke-Mooniyang-Montréal, they are the author of *Faire des enfants* (Leméac 2011); *Riverbed*, translated by Jordan Arseneault); *Ces regards amoureux de garçons altérés* (2015); and *L'Amoure Looks Something Like You* (Hamac 2022). They are also the author the children's theatre pieces *La Mère, le Père, le Petit et le Grand* (2012) and *Asteroid B 612* (Leméac 2021).

Rhiannon Collett (they/them) is a playwright, performer, and translator based in Vancouver on the territories of the Squamish, Musqueam, and Tsleil-Waututh Nations. They are interested in interdisciplinary creation processes, sexual labour, gender performativity, and science fiction. Selected playwriting credits include *Miranda & Dave Begin Again* (Playwrights Guild of Canada's RBC Emerging Playwright Award), *Wasp* (Nightswimming/safeword), *The Kissing Game* (Youtheatre/Young People's Theatre/Maison Théâtre), *J'ai Jamais* (French translation by Pénélope Bourque, Youtheatre/Télé-Québec/Maison Théâtre); and *Girlfriend* (Young People's Theatre).

In a gay bathhouse in Montréal, a tiny room becomes one man's confessional. Drugged to the bone, he's locked himself away for sixty hours, forever. His body is no longer his own, and his words, fuelled by crystal meth, are relentless. Amidst the chaos, he tells us—as best he can—of the last few years, of the last few hours. In the black hole of romantic grief, his head full and his heart broken, he struggles with his desire to disappear.

Our protagonist tells the story of the first time he and his ex-lover met, before the heartbreak, before his deep dive into self-destruction.

✦✦✦

The night I met Manu I was possessed by this desire,
throbbing like music,
like pain:
sleep with a new boy.
On my phone
the ever-present
parade of dark photos:
faceless bodies
dick pics
floating in space.
And then his profile:
A photo of his torso,
turned slightly to the side,
all the way to his neck,
his chin,
his lower lip.
He lived nearby,
we exchanged our measurements,
asked some questions,
he made a joke
I don't remember anymore,
a flash of wit,
but it made me smile.
Wittiness on Grindr is rare.

Then he sent me a photo of his face.
Too handsome,
I thought,
I don't stand a chance.
I sent my photo.
Waited.
He replied with four letters:
cute.

Cute.

I put on what I always put on.
The same briefs,
the same grey skinny jeans,
the same fitted T-shirt,
the one I look a little more muscular in.
New boys always say it makes my eyes look incredible.
Manu,
he wouldn't say that,
he'd never say it.
I didn't know then,
but trying to be beautiful for Manu
would make me ugly.
Uglier and uglier,
a failure.

Looking good for Manu was humiliating.

I walked,
head empty,
all the way to that soulless park on Darling Street.

I love my neighbourhood.
I love Montréal,
like everyone else.
I've lived here forever,
I mean since I left my family,
which is pretty much the same thing.
Adolescence and its prequel
were lost in the move.
All I have are some vague images,
drowned in family fiction and photographs.
My childhood is hard-shelled: uncrackable
enough to make any therapist drool.
A wasted time,
abandoned in my brain.
A snake left for dead at the bottom of a cave.

I want to throw myself at the world
again and again,
lose my naïveté,
all of it,
about what they say is beautiful:
peace, love,
childhood, old age.

The moment I meet Manu,
two choices appear:
Refuse to grow up or become respectable.
I had this premonition that if I let time do its thing,
life would close in on me, bit by bit.
That the sum of my experiences,
my classes,
my friends,
the parties,
the fucking,
would create an abyss that would swallow me whole.

I told myself that what was going to keep me alive,
save me,
reverse the trend,
was Love,
if it showed up,
if I accepted,
if it stayed.
Thanks to Love,
I could become respectable without hating myself
to death.

In that soulless park on Darling Street,
Manu and I,
kiss
for the first time,
our mouths full of whisky.
My knees give out,
Manu stops me from falling,
but I fall anyway.
I touch his cock through his jeans.
He takes my hand in his and drags our bodies out of the park.
We cross the train tracks,
we're going to dance.
Drink.
Take speed.

We walked a whole hour in the cold to get back to his place,
I went in,
and without knowing it, entered an ice palace.
All I thought of was his body,
couldn't see the moon reflected
in his many-mirrored room.

All night
and morning,
Manu will do the most beautiful things to you,
make you sink,
every night,
into the confusion of bodies and silence.

The orgasms came one after another,
but I wanted more.

My ass was complaining,
my head was light.

It felt like freedom
to let someone hurt me that much.
Turn the world on its head,
not sleep at night,
take drugs in public washrooms,
spend for no reason,
disinvest,
unlearn,
dance without modesty,
let a man I'd loved for less than three hours
stick three fingers up my ass on the dance floor:
all of that,
is happiness,
pure happiness.
Created artificially.
I thought:
Natural happiness doesn't exist,
if it did, we'd know about it.
I thought this and I told him.
The speed was making me talk.

All night,
I hammered him with questions.
He was inside me,
I was sitting on his dick and even then I couldn't stop:

Your last name?
Francophone?
On your mother or father's side?
And your father?
What language did you speak at home?
Do you know how incredibly beautiful your name is?

And at that he smiled,
and gave a big thrust.
I thought I could feel his dick all the way up to my sternum,
my eyes almost popped out of my head,
I grabbed his face in one hand,
his hair in the other,
I looked him right in the eyes—I wanted to cry from joy, from pain.
I smiled too,
and spat in his mouth.
He collected the spit with the tips of his fingers,
rubbed it,
on his fingers,
on his cock.
And with that I could go on.
He tortured me a while longer.
Sex with Manu is . . . was perfect:
it hurt so much I forgot the world.

Then Manu fell asleep,
of course.
And I didn't,
of course.
Manu was snoring before the sperm dried on the sheets.
He put his head on the pillow,
kissed me,
and he was gone:
when he woke up
he wasn't there.
Not like he'd been that night.
Before Manu fell asleep,
he was the love of my life.
Earlier on the dance floor,
we'd dreamt of our lives together,
the two of us,
I know that
for sure.

CHAPTER 7
WHAT'S IN A NAME?

THE RADICAL COLLECTIVISM OF GOOSE CULTURE

KAI FIG TADDEI

kai fig taddei (any pronouns) is a neurotic trans squiggle whose habits include deleting and reinstalling dating apps, forgetting about that tea they poured an hour ago, and catastrophizing. fig is a settler of mixed European ancestry, born and raised on the unceded territories of the lək̓ʷəŋən and W̱SÁNEĆ peoples, where he is currently studying law. she hopes you find something in this anthology that makes you slam it down on a table and shriek, YES!!!

C: Twenties to thirties. The performer can decide how (or if) the character defines their own gender.

✦✦✦

c: He's only misgendered me once, actually. In all the time we've been dating. One time. But it . . . when he did, I . . .

It was completely out of left field, too? We were having Thanksgiving dinner with his parents, who—have you met them?

They're nice. Mostly. A little scary. Like . . .

Rich people scary? I mean. They celebrate Thanksgiving. So . . .

So like, I was already a bit on edge, right? And Isaac was on edge, too, because. You know. It's a big deal! Meeting the parents, it's a big deal, right?

And his dad, his dad is this bald guy, this stern-looking bald guy, and his mom is like, capital-L Liberal, and—it wasn't like they asked if we were going to get married or anything, but his dad—his dad's a big birder. So there we are, sitting and eating this turkey and I dunno, celebrating genocide, I guess, and his dad starts going off about all these different bird species that mate for life. Which, turns out, is a lot of them? Like . . . Canada geese and bald eagles and osprey and scarlet macaws and—

I honestly don't even know why I remember this. Bird facts! Like, okay brain, you can remember what a scarlet macaw is, but not whether you took your hormones this week?

I think . . . I guess I wanted to make a good impression. Which I think sometimes means I, like . . . collect facts. About the people I need to like me. Try to memorize them—not just the facts, but. The people. Like. Commit them to memory. Because then I'll *know* them, right, and if I *know* them—their birthday, phone number, star sign, which credit union they bank with, the story of their first kiss—it's like I think if I know all *that*, I'll know *them*, and if I know *them*, I'll know how to make them love me forever and never ever ever leave me.

Beat.

So I'm sitting at this dinner table thinking his dad is trying to, like, convey his displeasure. Subtextually. You know, like: if aaaaall these birds can be monogamous, why can't you?

And that fucked me up, actually. Cuz later, I went and read more about birds, their mating habits, all that crap—and, turns out: complicated! Okay, like: Canada geese, right? Sure, they're kinda monogamous. But they don't do the whole isolationist model of monogamy we do. They don't pair off and take out a mortgage and then disappear from their friends' lives forever. They co-parent—child-rear as, like, a goose collective. Take turns watching the goslings, like in rotations, so all the adult geese still have time to fly off and take care of their goose needs and none of them become so burnt-out and resentful they "accidentally" drown their own babies.

Geese are *wise*.

But Isaac's dad isn't saying any of that. He doesn't talk about the radical collectivism of goose culture—no way. He makes it sound like Canada geese are out there living in nuclear geese families, policing who's fit to raise their own goslings and who's fit to adopt and who's so un-goose-like they don't even get to be part of the flock.

Isaac's mom isn't saying anything. Nobody's saying anything except his dad. We're just sitting stiffly around this gigantic table—this table that probably cost more than my rent for a whole month, this table that's so sanded down it's smooth and featureless, like it's not even made of wood—getting lectured in this passive-aggressive way about how Isaac and I choose to do our relationship even though it so completely none of his fucking business. And Isaac is stressed out, too, right, like obviously he's not *enjoying* this weird indirect criticism thing that's going on, so eventually he starts trying to interject, like interrupt his dad and change the topic or question what his dad is saying but his dad isn't having it, his dad just keeps talking, talks over him, not even looking at him, just methodically carving up this huge portion of turkey into perfect little squares of tender white meat until finally Isaac snaps and he says—

"She doesn't even want kids!"

Beat.

Ya.

So.

Beat.

It was only the one time. It was only the one time, it was a stressful situation, he wasn't thinking . . .

So. Why can't I let it go?

And then I spiral, right, like: what does it even matter? What does it matter if my partner fucks up my pronouns every now and then? I'm out, aren't I? I mean, my passport has a freakin' "X" on it! Like, would I even care this much if it was somebody else who screwed it up—a friend, or a co-worker . . .? Is it really fair to expect more of him just cuz, what—cuz we're dating?

But . . . after six *months*? Out of nowhere? It made it feel like . . . like it's always going to be in there. Somewhere. Deep inside him. This idea of me as . . . and maybe he's not conscious of it, but honestly? That scares me.

It's like . . . okay, I don't know what it actually feels like to be colorblind, obviously, but. It's like, with Isaac, I can say: Look. You see this, right? You see this? This is me. And he does, he does see me, but the thing is I'll never know if we're talking about the same me. I can never know that. What if the "me" I see is orange, but the "me" he sees is yellow, or blue, or—?

This is a shitty analogy. That's probably what he'd tell me, if he was here. "I love you, but that's a shitty analogy." Guess that's what I get for dating a cis guy.

I don't even mean that. I just said it cuz I thought it might make me feel better. Piling on cis people usually makes me feel better. But it's not like I haven't been misgendered by trans people. It's not like that doesn't bruise just as bad. Worse. It's not like *I* haven't ever . . .

Beat.

I've been thinking about what you said. Earlier. About how conflict—*choosing* conflict—that can be a privilege, too. Like how, even though in a lot of ways, Isaac's parents symbolize everything I think is fucked-up and immoral about our society, at the same time—they invited us into their home. They fed us. They didn't seem to care that I'm . . . whatever I am. Or if they did, they didn't let on. When we started dating, honestly, I couldn't wrap my head around why Isaac still talks to them, but . . . when he misgendered me—afterwards—I guess that relationship started to make more sense, too? Him and his parents. I know he's scared, there's not a second he's not scared about what might come out of their mouths next, but . . . he stays. He loves them. So. He stays.

Beat.

You're right. You're right!

It's obviously *waaaay* more complicated than that. Like the geese. It's not just unconditional love, is it? It's . . . something else.

WHAT'S IT ALL FOR

ZOË COMEAU

Zoë Comeau (she/her) is a bilingual Acadian theatre artist residing in K'jipuktuk (Halifax). Producer, director, writer, actor, and a proud absurdist, Zoë works hard to make sure that art happens. Since 2018, she has spent countless hours developing and working with other bilingual artists in Nova Scotia through her own theatre company, the Théâtre DesAssimilés. In addition to her own productions, Zoë has worked with various companies focusing on theatre and performance art aimed to challenge the status quo and getting audiences to see the world through a different lens.

Trans woman, aged twenty to forties, any ethnicity, highly educated. She has brought a man who sexually assaulted her to court, and they keep deadnaming her throughout the trial. The jury isn't leaning in her favour. This monologue is her last hurrah.

✦✦✦

ZOE: what is this for
i mean it.
what — or why — is this happening ?
i put my old name, my deadname as they call it, to rest .

why can't you follow suit .

is it curiosity ?
the search of something deeper ?
why can't you let it go .
drenched in desire or empathy ?
i honestly, and simply

don't know

why you can't
just
let it . the fuck . go .
i wish i could
but the taste of it on your tongue won't let me forget

falling into boredom so easily, pulling me into their idle minds and active imaginations .
how about you take a picture and go fuck yourself . i feel like i've lost the plot but i can't
move out of their way fast enough . all you want me to do is to buy a vowel so they see
how deep my throat goes and checking out my dick-sucking lips as the letter "o" drips
out of my mouth .

on the black market, my kidneys are worth 200 k. my liver — 157 k. heart — 119 k. skin — 10 per square inch. blood — 337 per pint. but you don't want any of it . you don't care about any of it . you aren't after money. hell, you're not even after my body .

you're after me.
my *queer* nature.

eyes grumbling, hands salivating, cock getting a little lightheaded .

maybe it's time to take a lesson from the greeks
castration creating Aphrodite
bloodshed creating beauty

you don't want my body, but you want what it can do . what it symbolizes . and what part of me does it for you exactly? hips swaying breathy voice soul bouncy tits big ass smooth legs smell of flowers small appetite dainty breakable hands porcelain skin barbie doll vagina

no
none of that shit .
looking for my lack of self-assurance , of validity .
the search for an emptiness you can fill with five and a half inches .

what a boring cliché .
so i broke it .
i broke you .
and it was fascinating .

— fuck i'm tired —

start a war . something personal . stay away from politics , but not politicians . make sure their eyes can't reach your skin ; but make sure you're close enough to bite theirs .

how did helen reduce troy to ashes
how did she remain serene ?
beautiful
blameless
beloved

zac died ,
and now zoe's a monster .

if heaven and hell exists
does god understand what it's like
to try to live and function
as prey

— day in day out —

does god know about inequality
does god care ?
the bible doesn't mention us
. . . oh but does it ever know about you
and you don't taste pure and blameless to me .

so how about we keep some pressure on that bloody lip i gave you
and tell god what happened
tell Him why

maybe He'll understand .
maybe He'll save you .
and if He does ,
then i guess this really was for nothing after all.

CHAPTER 8
BEYOND

ZAKA'AN

YOLANDA BONNELL

Yolanda Bonnell (she/they) is a bi/queer Two-Spirit Anishinaabe-Ojibwe, South Asian mixed performer, playwright, and multidisciplinary creator/educator. Originally from Fort William First Nation in Thunder Bay, Ontario (Superior Robinson Treaty territory), her arts practice is now based in Tkarón:to. She is co-artistic leader of manidoons collective, that she runs with Michif (Metis) artist, Cole Alvis. In February 2020, Yolanda's four-time Dora-nominated solo show *bug* was remounted at Theatre Passe Muraille while the published book was shortlisted for a Governor General's Literary Award. She won the PGC Tom Hendry Drama Award for her play *My Sister's Rage*, and has taught at schools like York University and Sheridan College. Yolanda proudly bases her practice in land-based creation, drawing on energy and inspiration from the earth and her ancestors.

It's the distant future: Land Back has happened. The land and body have begun to heal. Waaseyaaban, a young Indigenous radical femme, is rising to leadership of their community. They are looking for answers from their ancestors about how to lead, but since the time of peace, ancestors have gone back to rest. How can we travel back in time to learn from those who came before us? Zaka'an means to ignite, light, or set it on fire in Anishinaabemowin. I look at this in different ways—looking back at igniting the fires of revolution—burning the old ways to make way for new—igniting the fire within to go forward, but mostly it's about lighting the eighth fire in the Anishinaabe prophecy. The lighting of the eighth fire signifies a coming together as one.

Waaseyaaban, a young Indigenous femme, is sitting in their cabin by the ocean. They are rising to leadership within their community but are having doubts. They are looking for answers. Waaseyaaban has been trying to raise and contact their ancestors past, but since the time of peace ancestors have gone to rest. They continue to speak with the land and try and ride the winds of time to travel back in ancestral memory to find the answers.

✦✦✦

In the shifting starry expansive night

Where time is all and nothing,

Waaseyaaban's voice whispers:
The most radical thing we can do in the future is to love ourselves
Fully
And completely
The way our ancestors love us

The way in which we leave a path for those who come next
A trail for you to return to.

WAASEYAABAN sits in front of a fire, burning in the centre

Candles and medicine are placed around them

Behind them is a large window facing the ocean

The waves crash under the full moon.

WAASEYAABAN speaks to the ocean and to their ancestors.

The land responds

WAASEYAABAN: I gotta close my eyes for a minute
Just let me close my eyes a minute
I can hear Gramma telling me to go to bed because I'm falling asleep on the couch again
I'm not falling asleep
I am waking up

Her voice is from a past so long ago
It echoes back beyond generations of ancestors who fought wars so we could be here now

Wars
So we could be here now
So be here now

See I'm looking at that memory
That memory doesn't belong to me
I'm bouncing back
Skipping backwards through time
Going back so I can see ahead
I'm trying to see forward
Because I can't see the here and now, you know?
I need another perspective

I need to jump into the brain of a past version of me
An ancestral version of me
My mother's mother's mom
Or my great-great-auntie
I need to see the future through their eyes
What did they hope to see?
Is this what they envisioned?
This world, their fantasy?

Did we do right by you?
Answer me!

(disembodied whisper)
Answer me

I'm here to tell you that leadership is lonely.
I learned that from the faces of the leaders that I meet
I see it in our elders who were babies born on the streets

How do I know if I'm the right one to lead?
I was raised in the knowing that my power is strong
But how can I do this alone?

And I read all the scrolls, you know?
The texts—the words of our grandparents
Our long long LONG distant relatives
You documented them
They live in between books and bodies
Is that because they were there for you?

They showed up in your hours of need. They held you when you wailed about your dying planet.
They presenced themselves alongside you on your battlefields—out on the streets—taking back our rights—giving us back our freedoms

One
Piece
Of land
At
A time!
They were there
They were there, all those spirits
Those wild overwhelming energies
You existed in twisted times and always led the way and now

Where are you?

(disembodied whisper)
Where are you?

WAASEYAABAN *throws open the front door and stands outside*

The wind blows around them

They stand in it

I gotta close my eyes for a minute
Just let me close my eyes a minute
No no, Gramma, I was just resting them
Resting them
See?
I can rest well
I can sleep easy
I can tell my baby about the time before the tipi

About the great apocalypse that lasted hundreds of years
The time where our ancestral tongues were removed and our ceremonies buried
Where sickness ravaged our lands and bodies
The time where they separated the land *from* our bodies
The time of extraction
Extinction
Extinguishment
They dug us up from the land and encased us in glass
And these are just stories, see
These are now myths
Because as if

As if we could be torn down, dug up, encased and silenced
As if our power isn't strong enough
to blow through white men like the chinooks blow through the free, open landscapes that we now protect
As if the buffalo didn't come thundering back into the valleys
This is the power you've imbued us with
Inspiring that eighth fire to be lit
We are the children of your most wildest dreams
And you were the ones who planted our seeds

They touch the trees and bushes that surround their house

The growth is returning at a quickening pace
The land is healing
It feels like the last gasp of a giant wound closing
That first bit of scar tissue forming

We've stitched ourselves back together
And you've gone back
Is that it?

Do you
Do you need me to tell you all of this from where I am, cousin?
Do you need to hear that we've taken it all back?

That our solid sovereign hearts beat so loud now that the drum has returned?
Do you remember what it sounds like?
In the lodge?
Did they ever tell you what it sounded like?
In the lodge?
Because I want to send this deep beat back to you through time
I want you to hear it and know

I want you to hear it and have hope
I want you to hear it and presence yourself to me!

I need you to see
What we see

The fires of revolution made it possible for this to be
There are embers in our hearts
With the rise of community

But I get lost in your texts searching for more prophecy

The wake was long, Auntie
The wake was long and I know
I know you're tired

And I know you're behind me and inside of me and a part of me
And I want you to rest the way I can rest now

But I need to know if there's much further to go
Is it enough to know that we've stopped the roads?
And that the pipeline scars are beginning to close?
That the water is clean and clear when it flows?
The matriarchs know
Our bundles are lighter
We don't have to carry such a heavy load

A drum beat starts

Time and space collide

WAASEYAABAN *begins to see their ancestors from the past as lights*

As ripples

As glimmers off the water

As wind in the trees

In memory

Generations before

They reach for them—search for them—yell for them

There's red all around us
And not from the blood of our fallen siblings
But from the shine on our skin and the land in our hearts
We've taken it back from the handprints and dresses
From the long-term effects of colonial messes

That sacred tobacco-filled colour
led the way down the road that kept us connected to each other
Kept us reaching for each other
Cousin to sibling to sister to brother
Oshki misko minowe nagamowin gizhii wewidam
Madwe' gizhii wewidam
Inwewin, anishinaabemowin azhen izhi biinjidoon
Eya'!
Eya'!
Bizindam!
Noondan!
Gi-zaagi'in Nookomis
Gi-zaagi'in Nin-zigos

WAASEYAABAN sings to their ancestors

They then hold one hand up to the moon

(disembodied whisper)
I love you

Breath

The ancestors depart

WAASEYAABAN *slowly lets their hand fall*

They cover their heart

Breathless

I just gotta close my eyes a minute

Let me just
Close my eyes
And I will wait for you

In those beautiful waking dreams

The waves crash in response

The moon and stars expand

MEMENTO MORI: A SUPPORT GROUP FOR THE DEAD

TREVOR BARRETTE

Trevor Barrette (he/him) is a queer theatre-maker, performer, stage manager, and teacher based out of Tiohtià:ke (Montréal). Upon graduating from theatre school, he founded the award-winning KaleidoscopeMTL, for which he directed their ten productions, including seven of his own works and the Montréal Fringe Festival hits: *Captain Aurora*, *Captain Aurora II*, and *Memento Mori*. His work has been presented at the Segal Centre Academy, Centaur Theatre's Wildside Festival, PlayShed Theatre's WRK N PRGRSS, and CETM Inc.'s Next Wave Festival. As a performer, he has had the pleasure of working with the National Arts Centre, the Segal Centre, Centaur Theatre, Repercussion Theatre, Geordie Theatre, and Scapegoat Carnivale, among others. Trevor has proudly served his community as president of the Montréal English Theatre Awards and vice-president of the Quebec Drama Federation. Visit www.trevorbarrette.com for more information.

Memento Mori is a support group for the dead, an in-between for those not yet ready to step into the light. Written as a series of monologues, which can be intercut and presented in any order, *Memento Mori* is a one-act, site-specific piece about grief, redemption, and acceptance.

Michael, although only in his early thirties, is the longest-standing member of the group. In between meetings, Michael spends his time back on Earth, watching the world go by and trying to find his widowed partner. Well, today's his lucky day.

Memento Mori: A Support Group for the Dead was first produced by KaleidoscopeMTL, Montréal, on June 1, 2017, and developed with the support of Playwrights' Workshop Montréal's Young Creators Unit. It was performed by Chip Chuipka, Derek Johns, Patrick Keeler, Lior Maharjan, Leni Parker, and Alex Petrachuk, with Trevor Barrette; directed by Trevor Barrette; with assistant direction by Sarah Segal-Lazar; dramaturgy by Jesse Stong; lighting design by Jon Cleveland; and sound design by Devon Bate.

✦ MICHAEL'S SHARE ✦

MICHAEL: Hey. I'm Michael. I've been coming to these meetings for . . . God knows how long. Been dead a bit longer than that. Most of you have heard my spiel before, but I've been speaking with Mort and I've been thinking about people I had done wrong and took for granted. I've been thinking about forgiveness. I know I talk about him a lot, but I saw him today and he was happy.

They say it makes things harder, maybe it does, but I like going down there. To walk among the living. It makes no difference to them, really, we know that. I just like watching people going about their day-to-day. The grind, y'know? I don't feel anything particular about it when I do. Just leaves crunching. Snow slushing. It's nice. There's a calm there.

I used to go to see him, to find his face in the crowd. At first, I saw him everywhere. His smile, his walk, his way on other people. Thinking I'd passed him on the street, turning a corner, or in a shop. You know, basic mind fuck-ery. Sorry. But in the end, I was glad, always glad that he was never there, what would I do? Touch him? Kiss the nape of his neck? Sneak up and slip my hands in his jean pockets?

Where I'm at now, I look back and I know I wasn't good to him. When they— When I got the news. I was—mad. I hated myself. Even though they assured me it had nothing to do with me, that it runs in the family, I ignored them. I got arrogant.

I prayed. I did, I swear. I went to church and I prayed. I did the whole nine yards. I sat, I knelt, I stood. I "Amen"-ed and Baby Jesus was going to save my mortal soul, gosh darn it. I tried. But it was only the one time. Yeah, I get how He thought there was no commitment there, just a hookup, with Jesus.

Anyway, since church didn't work. I went out. 'Cause I couldn't go home. It got too quiet at home. I didn't want to talk about It. And he didn't either. And we couldn't seem to think of anything else to talk about, so instead of drowning in that quicksand silence, I went out.

I spent a lot of time on my own. Searching for . . . something. Something I didn't have. Something I thought I needed. I walked around. I went to the movies. I read at twenty-four–hour coffee shops. It was nice. I saw a lot of my friends, but eventually, all we talked about was It. So, I made . . . new friends.

I took myself out for a drink at a bar, this one guy, really, *so* not my type was—and, nothing happened, we talked, we just, talked, and it was cool, but it felt like something, something, small. And at that time, even for that "nothing," I hated myself. But I was feeling—still capable of feeling something good. And that meant something to me. So.

When I got home, I told him, about the bar, because deep down I felt, bad or whatever. But . . . he didn't react. He didn't— He heard what I was saying, what I had said and, it should have been a thing, a tiff, a talk, but . . . nothing.

So, I went out and, eventually, I did do something. And again. And again. And I kept at it, like I was filling some void, or quota. Missed opportunities. Like an erotic bucket list. Anything I wanted to do, everything I hadn't done, I just said. Well. Seize the day. Leave no box unchecked. So, I went and . . . started checking off those boxes. And it made me feel . . . full. And you want to die full.

And he just let me get away with it. So, I . . . got my freak on and he remained. I climbed into bed. I'd kiss him good night and he'd wake up in the morning, bring me my coffee, and I'd pretend to be asleep. And it was nice, but I just wanted to shake him. Make him feel something. Wake him up. Even though I still loved him, through all of our stupid, keeping this dead thing alive. I just wanted him to hate me and end it, so badly, because I couldn't . . . but I don't even know if that's what he would have wanted. And if for the rest of our lives if . . . if . . . But none of that really matters.

"It was only a matter of time." That's what they said. That seemed to be all we heard, all that remained of that ugly day. And he stood by me. Playing in my hair as it fell out. Holding me as I wasted away. Refusing to let me go.

Um. So, when I . . . let go, and came here, all I could think about was saying sorry. I hoped, dunno, but I wanted him to hear it. I said it in my head over and over and over again: "I'm sorry." "I'm sorry, I was confused." "I'm sorry, I didn't know what else to do, it just happened. I'm sorry, I—" I hoped that one day, some day, he'd hear it. In the wind. Off the tide. Something.

He cried at the funeral. I know you're not supposed to, but I had to go. He's the ugliest crier in the world. Really. It's . . . it's embarrassing, but it always made me smile, 'cause, obviously, I'm a dick.

But I saw him today, holding this guy's hand, and he was happy.

A PRACTICAL (IF DATED) TREATISE ON THE ART OF GENDERQUEER DANCING

CHRISTINA COOK

Christina Cook (she/they) is a theatre artist and therapist. Christina's writing credits include the play *Quick Bright Things*, published by Playwrights Canada Press and a finalist for the 2020 Governor General's Literary Award for Drama; and *Gerty*, half electronic-communication-from-the-future, half radio-drama-drag-show, and all genderqueer, published in *Educational Fabulations* (2022).

A Practical (If Dated) Treatise on the Art of GenderQueer Dancing is from a cycle of plays that collapses present, future, and past, blending historical fact with fiction and autobiographical with fantasy. Re-storying history, the play is set in a world where trans, non-binary, and gender-nonconforming individuals are recognized and celebrated in Canada in the early 1900s.

Ellis (they/them) is genderqueer, and can be played by an actor of any age. The actor playing Ellis should read the stage directions aloud as part of the monologue.

✦✦✦

July 1926
ELLIS *(they/them), genderqueer, holding a tattered book*
beside them, a sweet, lovely wall: this wall has a crannied hole
ELLIS *picks at the hole*
they speak through the hole, trying to reach me,
your stage directions
(you may read me aloud if you choose—and please choose to,
please read me aloud)
from my perspective as a stage direction, I'm very much
enamoured with ELLIS *and*
would, in fact, like to ask them to dance.
All that is stopping us is this wall, and
time.

So there you have it.

ELLIS: "THE AMATEUR'S VADEMECUM: A PRACTICAL TREATISE ON THE ART OF DANCING," by E.B. Reilley, 1870. My dear Grandpom-pom's, originally, lovingly bequeathed, and with practicality, of course—need it even be repeated? "COMPRISING THE MODERN HISTORY OF DANCING—THE ETIQUETTE AND FASHIONS OF THE—" WALTZ! OH MY, THEY HAVE WALTZES IN HERE, MY DEAR PYRIAS! Am I too loud? Forgive my exuberance, ah-ha? The dance, the dance—it gets into my throat and the floorboards. Ahem. Shhhh.

much quieter

"The conducting of parties, soirees, and the rudiments of classic and private"—PRIVATE!?—apologies, sh-sh-sh—"private dancing . . . and a brief"—but entirely thrilling, no doubt thrilling! Ah-ha!—"A brief-(thrilling)-essay on the importance of dancing, as an amusement, accomplishment and exercise." Ta-ta-ta! Watch.

ELLIS places the book on the floor
and proceeds to dance aerobically for several seconds, a solo
waltz of sorts
but with upper body movements that say "my pounding heart
could be the end of our world"
and also, "I might be hungry"
the movement climaxes and comes to stillness, ELLIS panting

Did you watch? Oh yes—no, of course—it is hard to make out anything through this blinking hole. The experiment was a success: Dance certainly is aerobic. I shall do it again for you later; I would like you to see it . . . if time allows.

picking up the book, licking their thumb, paging through it

Shall I begin with the essay? Shall I—

they stop, picking at the wall, then place their ear to it (to
me—call me Pyrias)—

No, no, you've nothing to fear. I choose my partner by elbow size alone, but I dance with all elbow sizes; I record them in the back of the vademecum for research. Elbow sizes, so far, are highly variable, and no conclusions, scientific or dance-related, can yet be drawn.

reading aloud, ELLIS waltzes, gently, through the following, as
they speak the steps from the book

"The circular movement of THE WALTZ has been compared to the motions of a planet in its orbit around its centre, as effecting a great circle by a number of smaller ones. Thus, every three steps constitute the half of a small circle, and their repetition completes that circle . . . When properly executed, it produces a very pleasing aspect, but the resulting dizziness constitutes an objectionable feature." But I, of course, am constantly dizzy and out of time, so I hardly notice.

What if Grandpom-pom could see us tonight, on the Grand Dance Pavilion? Would Grandpom-pom see both of us, or only me, thon's grandchild—Pom-pom used thon pronouns—standing alone amidst the orbiting partners. The posters claim the Pavilion fits eight hundred couples, any and all genders welcome.

by now, it must be clear that ELLIS *lives in a history I only see through a crannied hole*

I will not dance with any of those sixteen hundred, no matter what size of elbows. I would rather wait for word through a hole . . . Grandpom-pom believed the ghost of a lion haunted thon's every waking moment. I told thon I believe ghosts are not hauntings from the past but visitors from the future. Tourists of time reaching back to us to ask us—

ELLIS *almost begins to dance again but hesitates*

There is an assumption you need to move to dance, not so, not so. There's an assumption you need to have a body to dance, dear Pyrias, NOT SO. We can dance with only my body between us.

an eyelash falls on ELLIS*'s cheek, hovering, refusing time*
I am jealous of this lash
your eyelash, ELLIS*, I need its technique*

I imagine you travelled back to 1870 to write these directions for dancing, before travelling, here, now. You are my future traveller, aren't you? What did the future lion want of Grandpom-pom? Aa-ha. Lions, too, I suppose, require dance. Ahem. Will you ask me to—? May I ask you to—?

they don't finish
I can make out their dancing again, slower, slower, wrenching,
and, also, like rain, relief
they lie against the wall (me, Pyrias)
oh ELLIS, *dear* ELLIS, *will you dance with me?*

CONCLUSION

BILAL BAIG

It feels like I've been afraid my whole life. Like, I distinctly remember having a really hard time speaking up in class in elementary school because I was scared to use my voice. I would struggle to ask the teacher if I could go to the bathroom.

I was scared of stuff going on at home. Other people's rage made me scared.

I was scared of getting bullied in middle school, of being too visible, too much of a target. I was scared when some dude in high school threatened to beat me up.

Theatre school was terrifying. Like, not in a good way. It's so strange to think that someone like myself, who dealt with significantly low self-esteem all throughout adolescence, ended up choosing to attend an institution for three years that focused essentially on telling me what's wrong about me, and who I can't be. Three years of being shoved into monologues and scene studies and costumes and voice work that made no sense to my mind and body.

And then, in my early twenties, I accepted that I'm trans. And with that acceptance came more fear. The kind of fear that freezes you and disconnects you. Fear of just like, being, existing in public. I'd be late for everything because I'd have to talk myself out of my fear of leaving my apartment and going outside and getting harassed, which I'd always know was pointless to do because I'd always get harassed in some way anyways. And so I'm walking around, avoiding eye contact, trying to shrink, which is completely paradoxical given my 5'10" height, over 6' in my heel boots. I'd elicit such a range of reactions from such a range of people. Shock, disgust, confusion, anger, annoyance, laughter. From cis men, cis women, teenagers, children, other trans people sometimes.

I keep telling myself as I'm writing this: *a good thousand-word personal essay would have some twist around this point, something that switches up the energy or direction or something.*

But all I have is more fear.

As I've stepped deeper and deeper into my transness, I've become more and more visible. And I know very well the truth about more visibility; it leads to more violence. Visibility inspires visibility. Violence inspires violence. And as I get older, I accept more and more this cycle is maybe never going to change. It's never going to break. I accept more and more that I'm an active participant in this cycle.

When we tell our stories, we will be celebrated and ridiculed. We will be cherished and disregarded. We will ignite necessary conversations and fuel hatred.

And still, when we tell our stories, we dig inward and reach across. When we tell our stories, we shape our futures. Futures that certainly aren't only full of hope and possibility and empowerment.

Our mothers may keep their distance from us.

Our lovers may leave us.

Our employers may continue to disappoint us.

Our hookups may remind us of a shame we keep returning to.

Our faith may wobble.

Our hopes may wander.

Our dreams may never come true.

And still, I'm kinda just like . . . I really want to see my friends get older. I really want to experience art made by the weirdest freaks and outliers. I really want to be led by queer and trans artists who feel free enough to follow their guts and take risks and make messy mistakes. I want to be there when these artists ask questions that feel impossible to answer and still they wait for the answer. I want to be in a room where literally everyone is sitting on the edge of their seats. I want to witness, I want to listen, I never want to stop transforming.

I want to become my future self. I know that's inevitable, but I'm saying I want to become versus I'm going to become. I *want* to become my future self and ask her a million questions:

Here you are, right? Is this really happening? How did we get here?

How do you identify now?

How do you feel about being alive right now?

What do you remember about childhood? Do you remember losing track of time? Endless imaginary worlds. Does that feel right? Do you remember wanting to speak but then choosing not to?

How often do you reflect on the past? How often do you let yourself dream about the future? In this moment, what's on your mind?

How bad is the pain? How good is the pleasure?

What feels unforgettable? What feels legendary? What feels devastating?

What happened to all that fear? Did it go anywhere or did it just keep racking up? Did it transform into anything that feels a bit more manageable? Or are you so used to being afraid now that it just feels like nothing?

Can we talk about something that hurts less?

I don't have the right words with this next question but is it cool, or like, badass or something to know that you're still here?

Like, we actually can't be destroyed, right? Violence inspires violence, but our stories will live. The stories, the moments, the characters in this book will live. Sure, this book could get banned or whatever, but that doesn't mean it stops existing. Doesn't mean it can't be found. Doesn't mean a quiet, queer-curious kid in the suburbs won't stumble upon it. No one can take away that it happened. That we happened. That we are happening right now and we'll keep on happening. We'll keep on carving out space for ourselves amidst all the opposition. We'll keep on saying the same things over and over again if we have to. We'll keep on being relentless in our pursuit of truth despite our fears. Because, honestly, is there anything more queer than that?

Thank you to our queer and trans communities.

EVAN'S THANK YOUS

Special thanks to my incredible mother Dimitra Argiros, Alexandra Tsitsias-Rotskas (forever in my heart and soul), Georgia Tsitsias-Fineman, Aaron and Joshua Fineman, Kevin Grillo, Mark Allan, Donna Marie Baratta, Shelly Meichenbaum, Sue Dunstan, Chang Nai Wen, Lisa Baylin, Rob Bauer, and all the others who listened to me talk incessantly about this project. Also a huge thanks to Annie Gibson and Blake Sproule, whose generosity, support, trust, and creativity are immeasurable.

ABOUT THE EDITORS

Evan Tsitsias (he/him) is co-artistic director/co-founder of Directors Lab North and the former artistic director of Eclipse Theatre Company. His writing includes *Aftershock*, *The Murmuration of Starlings*, *Unstuck*, *Strange Mary Strange*, *Inge(new)—In Search of a Musical*, and the short film *Bagged*, which aired on the CBC. He's worked internationally as a writer, director, performer, and teaching artist and spent the last decade in Houston at Theatre Under the Stars. He is a member of the Lincoln Theater Center Directors Lab, Chicago Directors Lab, the Tarragon Playwright's Unit, Stratford Festival's New Play Development Program, and was a resident artist at Robert Wilson's Watermill Center. He's been nominated for a Dora Mavor Moore Award, the John Hirsch Director's Award, the Tom Hendry Award, and received Honourable Mention for the Voaden National Playwriting Prize. His book *The Directors Lab* was published by Playwrights Canada Press in 2019. His work has also been published in several anthologies in Germany, Canada, and the USA. Visit www.evantsitsias.com for more information.

Bilal Baig (they/them) is a queer, transfeminine, Muslim playwright, performer, and workshop facilitator. Bilal's first play, *Acha Bacha*, had its world premiere in 2018 and has been published by Playwrights Canada Press. Other written work in development includes *Kainchee Lagaa*, *Kitne Saare Laloo Yahan Pey Hain*, and *I want that free mind!* Bilal is a core team member at non-profits such as Story Planet and Rivers of Hope, where they develop and facilitate workshops for youth in under-resourced neighbourhoods in Toronto focused on creative writing and literacy (Story Planet) and combatting Islamophobia through the arts (Rivers of Hope). Bilal has been the Playwrights Unit Facilitator for the Paprika Festival since 2019. Bilal is the lead and co-creator of the CBC/HBO Max/Sienna Films series *Sort Of*.